Design

'...Another squint through the binoculars...No. It couldn't be true. I looked again, straining hard. Surely I must be wrong. Someone muttered 'Heaven next stop'. I realised that my guess was right. There were only two ships in the world that even remotely resembled the foremost of the two strangers – the giant battleships Nelson *or* Rodney*!'*

(ADC Ulrich Mohr,
German Raider *Atlantis*, 18 May 1941)

As attested to by Ulrich Mohr as he stood transfixed in horror on the bridge of the raider *Atlantis*, the British battleships *Rodney* and *Nelson* were, and still are, the most instantly recognisable battleships in history. Britain's only dreadnoughts to carry 16in guns, possessors of a unique silhouette with three main gun turrets all grouped forward and a massive control tower amidships, the two sisters could never be mistaken for any other battleship. From a viewpoint nearly a century later where we are used to the sleek and modern looking battleships that came after them, they appear old-fashioned, ponderous, perhaps even ugly, but that impression overlooks what they really were. Brilliantly innovative in concept and design, unmatched by their contemporaries, and superior to most battleships that came after them, HMS *Rodney* and HMS *Nelson* are among the most successful battleships ever constructed.

Although victorious in the Great War, the Royal Navy in 1919 faced the prospect of being outgunned by new ships building in the US and Japan. A reluctant Admiralty turned its attention to building new battlecruisers and battleships that would be far in advance of anything even remotely proposed by any rival navy in terms of main armament, armour, and speed. The innovative team of battleship design chief E L Attwood and his deputy Stanley Goodall came up with the novel idea to concentrate all the armament forward. This allowed the ship's vital areas of main armament, magazines, machinery, and boilers to be grouped together, reducing the length of the armoured citadel and providing the key to supplying adequate armour protection.

The legendary 48,000-ton 'G3' battlecruisers with nine 16in guns and the equally legendary 48,000-ton 'N3' battleships with nine 18in guns were the result. Both designs were far and away the best dreadnoughts of their time; only the later *Yamato* and *Montana* classes had thicker belt armour, and only the *Yamato* class had thicker deck armour. The 'G3's were laid down in November 1921 but the Washington Naval Conference which convened the following month was to set an upper limit on battleship construction of 35,000 tons and 16in main armament. The 'G3's were cancelled as they were way over the new limit, but Britain was allowed to

Below: *Nelson* on 17 May 1937 at the Coronation Fleet review. Her unique profile contrasts sharply with the more conventional *Queen Elizabeth*s in the background, giving some idea of the impression these highly unusual battleships made when they first entered service. Since completion the DCT platform has been extended and she is still carrying the single HACS Mk I on the AA platform. Note the neutrality stripes and the letters 'NE' on 'X' turret (this is sometimes called 'C' in published sources but 'X' was the official designation). The sponson at the base of the bridge tower can be seen clearly in this view as is the straight crane boom. The top of the mainmast is painted much lighter than the rest of the mast. *(By courtesy of Ray Bean)*

Above: *Nelson* in her 'as built' condition prior to any modifications. Note the single 2pdr AA guns on the conning tower platform walkway, the double row of bridge windows, the signalling projectors on the bridge tower, and the life rafts stowed on and ahead of 'X' turret. There is also a large wooden sailing ship model on the weather deck just below the AA guns. *(By courtesy of Ray Bean)*

build two new ships to the new limits to counter the 16in-gunned USS *Maryland* and the Japanese *Nagato*.

DESIGN & CONSTRUCTION

After the preliminaries of the Washington conference when it became apparent that a fixed upper limit of 35,000 tons was going to be set, sketch designs were prepared for two battlecruisers with 15in guns and a speed of 29.5kts. These were rejected as a main armament of 16in guns was desired in order to match the *Maryland* and *Nagato*. It quickly proved impossible to meet the demands for such a heavy armament, high speed, and adequate protection on the limited tonnage. The requirement for high speed was dropped and the focus shifted to a battleship design. The new requirements were ready by December 1921 and called for ships of 35,000 tons with nine 16in, a 13-14in main armour belt, deck armour of 4in to 10in, a high freeboard, and a speed of 23kts.

In order to meet the design requirements for protection, the designers borrowed from the 'G3' concept and concentrated the main armament forward instead of fore and aft. This greatly reduced the length of ship that had to be protected. For the first and only time in British battleships, the engine rooms were placed forward of the boiler rooms in order to have the funnel as far away from the bridge as possible. The secondary armament of 6in guns was grouped together at the after end of the superstructure. The result was the distinctive silhouette of the *Nelsons*, flush-decked with a very high freeboard, three main gun turrets forward, the superstructure with its single funnel and a cluster of 6in turrets concentrated aft.

Armour. The main armour belt extended from the forward end of 'A' barbette to the aft end of the 6in magazines, a distance of 384ft. This was an internal belt and was angled at 72°, sloping inwards from the top of the hull, the top being supported by the armoured deck. The bottom edge rested on a shelf which sloped inwards from the bottom of the ship at an angle of 30°. Any direct hit on the belt would tend to try and push the belt up this slope, locking it even more firmly into place. The belt armour itself was 13ft high. It was 14in thick abreast the main magazines under the main gun turrets and the forward control spaces under the bridge tower. It was 13in thick abreast the machinery spaces and the 6in magazines.

The forward end of the belt armour was

Right: *Rodney* prior to any modifications with two rows of bridge windows, signalling projectors fitted, no blast deflectors, and a very wide yardarm at the masthead. *(By courtesy of Ray Bean)*

Left: A very good view showing many details of *Nelson* in 1927–1930 prior to any modifications. The projector platform signalling lights, two rows of bridge windows, torpedo rangefinder towers, the AA platform and the unshielded 4.7in guns, boat crane boom rigging, boat davit rigging, and the two boats in the water are all shown to good advantage. *(By courtesy of Ray Bean)*

closed off by a 12in thick armoured bulkhead that ran across the ship connecting to the belt armour on both sides. The bottom of this bulkhead tapered to 8in at the bottom of the ship and protected the magazines from end-on fire. At the after end of the belt armour, a 10in armoured bulkhead closed off the belt armour. The combination of the belt armour and the two armoured bulkheads at each end of the main belt created an armoured box or citadel that completely protected the ship's vitals. At the very after end of the ship, another 4in thick armoured bulkhead protected the steering gear. There was no other protection at all outside of the citadel.

The top of the armoured box was the armoured deck at the middle deck level. It was 6¼in thick from the forward armoured bulkhead to the forward bulkhead of the engine room. From there over the machinery spaces to the after armoured bulkhead it was 3¾in thick. It was 4½in thick from there to within 25ft of the stern in order to protect the steering gear. It should be noted that this deck was armoured, not merely protective plating. This was the first time in British battleships that an armoured deck had been fitted, and it is possible that the *Nelsons* were the first battleships in the world with a true armoured deck.

The main barbette armour was 15in thick at the sides, tapering in thickness towards the middle of the ship. The main turrets had 16in thick armour plates on the front faces, with 9in sides and a 7in roof. The conning tower had 14in sides, 12in front, and a 10in rear. The revolving hood seen in front of the bridge had plating 3in thick. The funnel uptakes between the armoured middle deck and the main deck were protected by four armoured tubes averaging 8in of thickness.

After testing it was concluded that the belt and 6¼in deck would withstand the impact of a 16in shell. If a 16in shell hit the 3¾in deck over the machinery spaces, the likelihood of a complete penetration and burst inside were considered remote. Total armour was 29.3% of the standard displacement and made *Rodney* and *Nelson* the most heavily protected battleships ever built until the advent of the Japanese *Yamato* class.

Anti-torpedo system. This was outboard of the main armour belt and extended down to the bottom of the ship. Seen in cross-section, it was a layered 'sandwich' consisting of the outer hull plating, an outer air-filled compartment, an inner water-filled compartment and a 1½in longitudinal protective bulkhead 12ft in from the side of the ship. The water-filled compartment was meant to be filled with some 2850 tons of water. This was only done during the war and increased the draught by 23 inches and cost a third of a knot in speed.

The double bottom compartments were 5ft high to give the greatest possible protection from a mine or torpedo detonating under the hull. The magazines were placed below the shell rooms so that if they were breached from below by a mine or torpedo, they would quickly flood.

Main armament. Some £500,000 had been spent developing the 16in Mk 1 gun for the cancelled 'G3's so it was desired to use the same gun for the *Nelsons*. It had been decided that a combination of a lighter shell with a higher muzzle velocity would result in greater penetrative qualities than the existing 13.5in and 15in guns, but this proved to be a mistake. During testing it was found that the light shell with its short body and long nose banged heavily against the rifled liner of the gun barrel causing rapid liner wear and a considerable loss of

THE 15in AND 16in GUNS COMPARED

Gun	Shell Weight (pounds)	Muzzle Velocity	Life of Barrel	Range	Weight of revolving structure
MK II 15in	1920	2450fps	350	30,500yds	860 tons
Mk I 16in	2048	2700fps	200	41,983yds	1480 tons

accuracy. The muzzle velocity was reduced in order to cure the problem.

Triple mountings were adopted to carry the maximum number of guns on the hull length. This was a novel mounting arrangement for the Royal Navy and they caused considerable trouble when first placed in service. The grouping of all three mountings forward allowed for maximum protection and actually helped simplify fire control at the expense of having no turret that could bear directly aft. The mountings themselves were very heavy at 1500 tons each and this great weight distorted the horizontal rollers that they revolved on. This was corrected by the addition of vertical rollers that took some of the lateral thrust off the horizontal rollers.

When all three guns were fired together, the middle shell affected the ballistic trajectory of the outer two shells, reducing accuracy, so the middle gun was not fired at the same time as the wing guns. However, all three barrels had to be loaded together. This resulted in a firing cycle of 65 seconds rather than the designed 30 seconds. Experience with the guns mounts eventually decreased the firing cycle, and *Rodney* attained rates of 1.6 salvos per minute against *Bismarck*.

There were a great number of complicated interlocks in the ammunition and powder charge loading systems as a precaution against flash. As a consequence it took many years of extensive experimentation to develop smooth procedures for loading and firing the guns. It was not until December 1934 that solutions were worked out for most of the loading and firing problems, but even then the mountings were never completely trouble-free.

When 'A' and 'B' were fired on forward bearings, there was damage to the deck fittings and being in the mess decks underneath them was deemed 'uncomfortable'. When 'X' was fired abaft the beam, conditions on the bridge were 'extremely uncomfortable'. During firing trials aboard *Rodney* in September 1927, it was noted that when 'B' was fired abaft the beam conditions were tolerable, but when 'X' was fired at 130° abaft the centreline there was considerable shock. Interestingly, the team in the DCT above the bridge reported no difficulties. Andrew Cunningham, the future CinC of the Mediterranean fleet during the Second World War and *Rodney*'s captain in 1930 summed up the problem: 'With the after turret on its extreme after bearing and the guns at considerable elevation ... it was possible from the bridge to see quite 10ft down the bore of the nearest gun.'

Further firing trials were held aboard *Rodney* off the Isle of Wight on 24–25 November 1930 after fitting blast deflectors and small pane glass to the windows on the compass platform. In the words of Captain Cunningham 'it was a complete failure. The bridge was indeed untenable through bits of flying plate glass from the completely shattered windows.' Fitting blast deflectors and plating over the upper row of bridge windows did help, but firing abaft the beam was restricted during peacetime. It was suggested that the bridge crew use the conning tower when firing.

The gun mountings had 40° of elevation which resulted in a range of 41,983yds. The larger shell was felt to be more effective at longer ranges than the 15in gun, the bigger shell splashes presumably being easier to

Below: A great picture showing the sheer menace of nine 16in guns poised for action. *(By courtesy of Ray Bean)*

Left: *Rodney* prior to any modifications, showing the open admiral's bridge and 16in tompions bearing the ship's badge. *(By courtesy of Ray Bean)*

see. During the war barrage directors were fitted which allowed the main armament to be used for long range fire against attacking torpedo bombers.

Secondary armament. In a radical departure from previous designs, the secondary armament was mounted in turrets, twelve 6in/50 Mk XXII guns being fitted in six Mk XVIII twin turrets. They were watertight and were physically mounted much higher above the waterline than in previous designs, which meant that the guns could be worked in much rougher seas. They also provided protection from splinters and the elements for the crews.

They were placed as far aft as possible to avoid blast from the main guns and to keep their magazines more compact, but the close clustering raised fears of all of them being disabled by a single hit. There was no weight left over to protect these mountings and they only had 1in of high tensile plate. The magazines were behind the 13in main armour belt and the ammunition supply chain had multiple interlocks for protection against flash.

The guns had a range of 25,600yds at

Left: An undated view of *Nelson*'s port side 6in turrets. The linoleum cover on the turret roof can be clearly seen on the lower turret. *(By courtesy of Ray Bean)*

45° of elevation and could be elevated to 60° for use against aircraft. Designed rate of fire was 7–8 rounds per minute, but 4 rounds per minute was the best initially achieved. As with the main guns, improvements and familiarity with the mountings eventually increased the rate of fire, *Rodney* attaining 5.9 rounds per minute during the *Bismarck* action.

Anti-aircraft armament. The main AA weapons were six single Mk VIII 4.7in unshielded guns. Four were installed amidships on the shelter deck; the other two were on the quarterdeck right aft. None of them could track across the bow, but all six could fire directly aft. At 90° of elevation they could reach 32,000ft. At low level targets their range was 16,100yds at 45°.

The ships were designed to carry four 8-barrelled 2pdr pom-poms, but these were not ready when the ships were completed, so eight single 2pdr guns were installed instead, four on the conning tower platform, and four right aft on the shelter deck.

Torpedoes. Two 24.5in torpedo tubes were fitted, one on each side forward of 'A' turret below the waterline, facing forward but angled slightly outboard. The 24.5in tubes were the largest torpedo tubes ever fitted aboard British ships and were unique to *Rodney* and *Nelson*. The torpedo size was ideal as it was shorter than a standard 21in torpedo, making it much easier to manhandle the torpedo bodies down to the torpedo flat. Ten to twelve torpedoes were carried, each weighed 5628 pounds with a 750-pound warhead. Range was 30,000yds at 30kts with a running time of 20 minutes, or 15,000yds at 35kts with a running time of 12.85 minutes.

ORDNANCE CHARACTERISTICS

Weapon	Maximum Elevation	Horizontal Range	Vertical Range	Rate of Fire RPM	Shell Weight (pounds)
16in/45 Mk I	40°	41,983yds	N/A	1.5	2053
6in/50 Mk XXII	60°	25,600yds	N/A	8	100
4.7in/40	90°	16,100yds	32,000 feet	8	50
2pdr pom-pom	80°	3,800yds	13,000 feet	90	2
24.5in torpedo	N/A	15,000yds at 35 knots 30,000yds at 30 knots	N/A	12 torpedoes	750

Propulsion/steering. Uniquely for British battleships, the engine rooms were placed forward of the boiler rooms, resulting in long propeller shafts. The disadvantage of longer shafts was more than offset by these features: the engine rooms could be built in a wider section of the hull giving better protection and the funnel uptakes could be moved further away from the main magazines and the bridge. There were two engine rooms to port and two to starboard, separated by a longitudinal bulkhead on the centreline. The four boiler rooms had an identical arrangement. Each engine room contained two turbines; each boiler room contained two boilers. All machinery compartments were isolated from each other, allowing independent use in case action damage disabled one or more compartments.

Design machinery output was 45,000shp for 23kts at 160rpm. Both ships could attain 16kts at 14,350shp at 100rpm. It took another 31,000shp to attain the extra 7kts to make top speed. *Nelson* made 23.55kts at standard displacement on trials in May 1927. *Rodney* made 23.8kts at standard displacement on trials in September 1927.

The twin-screw arrangement was also unique for British dreadnoughts, two larger screws being thought to provide more manoeuvrability than four smaller ones. The single rudder was fitted on the centreline and was controlled by a new type of electro-hydraulic system with rams operated by oil under pressure from three variable-speed pumps powered by an electric motor. The turning circle was less than 700yds.

One captain stated that they were much easier to handle in calm weather than the preceding *Queen Elizabeth* and *Royal Sovereign* classes and had better astern power than the *Queen Elizabeths*. Another stated that if the superstructure was thought of as a fully set mizzen sail and the steering was adjusted accordingly, then there were no real difficulties. Captain Cunningham reported of *Rodney*: 'But beyond the remoteness of the stem and a majestic dilatoriness in answering her helm and propellers, I eventually found her little different from the smaller ships to which I had been accustomed.'

Bridge tower. The tower bridge structure was an important innovation, designed to do away with the old-style heavy tripod foremast with bridge details built around it as seen in all previous British dreadnoughts. The new structure was primarily chosen to give solid support to the main and secondary DCTs, which had to be carried as high in the ship as was possible. It also gave increased protection to personnel by reducing draughts, reduced the amount of funnel smoke drawn into the bridge area, and provided much needed office and cabin space.

It had a few disadvantages in that bridge personnel did not have an all-round view, the admiral's bridge was crowded, signals flying from the mainmast could not be seen from the compass platform, and at slow speeds it acted like a sail. These were minor problems; there had been much more criticism about the older style heavy tripod arrangement. A similar tower bridge structure was repeated for the *King George Vs*, *Vanguard*, and the reconstructed *Queen Elizabeths* and *Renown* so it can be safely assumed that it was a success.

Fire control. The main armament was controlled by two DCTs, one atop the main tower structure and the other at the after end of the shelter deck, each with a 15ft rangefinder. The secondary armament was controlled by four DCTs, each having a 12ft rangefinder. Two were carried abreast the main DCT atop the main tower structure, with the other two just forward of the after main DCT on the shelter deck. There was also an alternative fire control position inside the armoured hood directly in front of the main tower structure. Each main turret had a 41ft rangefinder as a backup for the main DCTs. Two 9ft tactical rangefinders were on the DCT platform as well.

The anti-aircraft control position for the 4.7in AA armament was located on the AA platform carried above the bridge tower. It originally consisted of a single high angle director in both ships. This was later replaced with an improved High Angle Control System, or HACS. *Rodney* only ever carried one HACS and could thus only control the 4.7in AA on one side of the ship at a time.

There were two torpedo rangefinder towers fitted abreast the funnel, one on each side, incorporating a 15ft rangefinder. A torpedo sight was also fitted on each side of the admiral's bridge.

Ship's boats. As a private ship: 2 x 50ft pinnaces, 1 x 35ft motor pinnace, 2 x 45ft motor launches, 2 x 32ft sailing cutters, 2 x 27ft whalers, 1 x 30ft gig, 2 x 16ft skiff dinghies. As a flagship were added: 1 x 30ft gig, 1 x 50ft admiral's barge, 1 x 13.5ft balsa raft.

All the boats were stored between the funnel and the mainmast and were handled by the main derrick attached to the forward side of the mainmast.

Miscellaneous. Six 18in signal projectors were carried on the bridge tower behind concealing flaps. Four 36in searchlights were carried, two on the funnel and two on the mainmast.

There were no topmasts or yards fitted on the bridge structure. The prominent

Above: A close-up of *Rodney*'s bridge tower as completed, taken on 24 August 1929, showing the two rows of bridge windows. It gives a good idea of the massive size of the main DCT on top. Note the single 2pdrs on the CT platform. *(By courtesy of John Roberts)*

Left: *Rodney*'s quarterdeck looking forward, 24 August 1929, with three of the ship's gun calibres represented – the twin 6in to port and starboard, two single unshielded 4.7in AA between them, and two single 2pdr pom-poms on the shelter deck above. Note the deck ventilators painted in a darker colour at their bases. *(By courtesy of John Roberts)*

Above: *Nelson* in August 1930 showing the forward port side 6in turrets, the aftermost of the 4.7in open mountings on the shelter deck, the torpedo director tower, and a ship's boat. The linoleum cover is not evident on the 6in turret tops in this view. *(By courtesy of John Roberts)*

lattice work projections seen at the front of the bridge tower and at the front of the AA platform were spreaders for the W/T aerials. The tripod mainmast had a derrick rigged on the front for hoisting the ship's boats.

The maximum weight was given over to protection and the main armament, which meant strict weight-saving measures everywhere else. Douglas fir was used instead of teak for the weather deck and there was extensive use of aluminum for internal fittings such as kit lockers, cupboards, mess racks, etc. After the design was approved, it was decided to use 'D' steel for the hull plates. This was a new type of steel with higher tensile strength than regular mild steel which meant that lighter plates could be used. The use of these thinner plates resulted in the ships being some 1500 to 2000 tons lighter than designed. This was an embarrassing oversight as the extra weight could have been used to provide better protection or to make the hull and superstructure stronger and less vulnerable to blast damage.

The crew's accommodation was well received, with plenty of natural light, ample headroom, and adequate ventilation. There were reading and recreation rooms, drying rooms for wet gear, a bakery, galley, laundry and electric ovens. The ventilation would prove to be inadequate for tropical service, a fault common to many British ships of the time.

The ships were well designed to fit within the treaty limits and had many innovations. Their design speed was 2kts faster than any contemporaries, and they would be the only battleships in the world to benefit from war experience until the advent of the French *Dunkerque* in 1937.

Their resemblance to contemporary oil tankers led to the nicknames 'Nelsol' and 'Rodnol'. The high tower structure resem-

Right: *Rodney* between 1932 and 1936 with the signalling projectors still in place in the bridge tower. The sponson and bridge cutout are evident along with the rangefinder at the back of the DCT platform. *(By courtesy of Ray Bean)*

CONSTRUCTION

Ship	Laid Down	Launched	Completed	Commissioned	Builder	Cost
Nelson	28.12.1922	3.9.1925	.6.1927	15.8.1927	Armstrong	£7,504,055
Rodney	28.12.1922	17.12.1925	.8.1927	8.11.1927	Cammell Laird	£7,617,799

bled an apartment block, hence the shared nickname 'Queen Anne's Mansions'. Being a cut down version of the 'G3's as a result of the Washington treaty they were also called the 'Cherry Tree Class'. And when looked at together, they did resemble a 'Pair of Boots'.

Construction. Design work was started in November 1921, and completed by 16 October 1922. Tenders were invited and those of Cammell Laird at £1,563,000 and Armstrongs at £1,479,000 were accepted on 1 November 1922. Both ships were laid down on 28 December 1922 with official ordering on 1 January 1923. *Nelson* was launched on 3 September 1925 and completed in March 1927 at a standard displacement of 33,313 tons. *Rodney* was launched on 17 December 1925 and completed in August 1927 at a standard displacement of 33,350 tons.

Nelson's steam trials were carried out on the Polperro Mile off West Looe, Cornwall in May 1927. She was commissioned at Walker on Tyne on 9 August 1927 and handed over by the builders the next day. She was brought to full commission at Portsmouth on 15 August and on 21 October, the 122nd anniversary of Trafalgar, Sir Hubert Brand, CinC Atlantic Fleet, hoisted his flag.

Rodney carried out her steam trials in the same location as *Nelson* in September 1927. She returned to Birkenhead for completion and was commissioned on 8 November 1927. She sailed for Portland in February 1928 to await the arrival of the Atlantic Fleet from the annual spring cruise.

Above: *Nelson* in 1934 showing the companionways at the back of the bridge tower. The starboard sponson and pom-pom have been fitted and the bridge signalling projectors are still in place. *(By courtesy of Ray Bean)*

CRITICISM OF THE DESIGN

At the time of completion, the ships were judged satisfactory except for the lack of any heavy astern fire, and insufficient depth of armour belt below the waterline. Over time other problems would become more apparent. It must be stated that such a radical new design could have been expected to exhibit some shortcomings, but with the exception of steering gear problems *Rodney* and *Nelson* were very successful ships.

Shallow main armour belt. The ships were vulnerable to diving shells and a proposal was made to deepen the main belt during a modernisation refit, but this was never carried out. It would require a far greater tonnage than allowed under the treaty limits to provide adequate protection against this menace.

Main Armament. The unsuccessful combination of a light shell/high muzzle velocity was the result of a flawed series of tests during development of the gun. This was corrected by reducing the amount of the propellant charge.

There were many teething problems with the triple mounting, mainly due to the numerous built-in safety features to prevent against flash reaching the magazines. These problems were mostly rectified during extensive trials in the 1930s as more experience was gained with the mounting.

Torpedo tubes. The torpedoes were of limited usefulness and their directors were removed in the 1930s. The torpedo flat was located outside the armoured citadel and the detonation of some 4.5 tons of high explosive would have caused massive damage had the torpedo compartment ever been breached by a heavy shell.

Steering. Both ships were slow to answer the helm and the high bridge tower acted like a sail when a wind was blowing. In consequence both ships handled badly, requiring a large amount of helm to keep them on a straight course. Steering was particularly bad at less than 7 or 8kts or when going astern. One officer reported that the ships were never under complete control when proceeding at less than 10kts. It was determined in testing after *Nelson* ran aground in January 1934 that the force of the wind against the superstructure was greater than the force of the rudder and the screws at slow speeds.

Above: *Nelson* after her 1940 refit and repair loading 16in shells. The 4.7in guns are shielded and the crane is in use. The sheer size of the main armament is shown by the crewmen lounging inside the apertures of the 16in guns. *(By courtesy of Ray Bean)*

Below: *Nelson* as completed, demonstrating the smoke interference with the bridge areas suffered by the ships in some conditions. *(US Navy)*

The rudder was undersized, was not of sufficiently heavy construction, and was not placed directly behind either of the propellers. It was this design defect that caused the continual steering problems, much more so than the large superstructure.

Nelson's rudder was reinforced, but this was not carried out on *Rodney* and her rudder almost completely tore away in December 1939. After this incident the CinC noted that the design of the rudder was too weak to stand the strain of rough seas and constant zig-zagging. *Rodney* in particular was to suffer many steering breakdowns during the war.

Blast. The 16in guns caused considerable damage when fired, particularly abaft the beam. Unlike conventional fore and aft armament layouts, the absence of any rear-facing mount meant that the forward turrets had to be trainable through considerable stern arcs. This was a consequence of the design, not a flaw with the ship itself.

Funnel smoke. The separation of the bridge and funnel was about 40ft, considerably further than in earlier designs, but it was not enough. The funnel was too short and when steaming directly into the wind, the bridge structure created a back draft which drew the funnel gases forward, making life uncomfortable. Plans to increase the height of the funnel or to add a cowl were made but neither improvement was ever carried out.

Weight saving. The strict measures applied to saving weight during design and construction meant that the structure of the ships was not as robust as it could have been. This was partly responsible for the extensive blast damage suffered when firing the main guns. Had it been anticipated that the use of the new 'D' steel would have resulted in such weight savings, the superstructure could have been made stronger.

Many measures taken to save weight in the machinery spaces (such as fewer onboard spares and reduced workshop capability) meant long term machinery problems, particularly for *Rodney*. *Rodney* suffered so many mechanical breakdowns that she became known by the unflattering nickname of 'Rodney Last'.

Left: Arranging all the main armament forward provided the opportunity for some striking and unique images of a battleship's power. A peacetime photo, note the highly polished muzzles of the gun barrels. *(By courtesy of John Roberts)*

DESIGN CHARACTERISTICS AS COMPLETED

Dimensions ***Nelson*:**

Length:		710ft
Beam:		106ft
Draught:	Standard	26ft 8in
	Extra Deep	30ft 6in
	Extra Deep	32ft 5in with torpedo protection filled

***Rodney*:**

Length:		710ft 2in
Beam:		106ft
Draught:	Standard	26ft 8in
	Extra Deep	30ft 6in
	Extra Deep	32ft 5in with torpedo protection filled

Armament

9 16in/45 Mk I in three triple mountings Mk I
12 6in/50 Mk XXII in six twin mountings Mk XVIII
6 4.7in/40 Mk VIII in six single mounts Mk XII
8 2pdr pom-poms in single mounts
4 3pdr Hotchkiss saluting guns
5 0.303in single Vickers machine guns
5 0.303in twin Lewis machine guns
4 0.303in single Lewis machine guns
2 24.5in torpedo tubes

Vertical Armour

Main belt:	14in to 12in
Armoured bulkhead forward:	12in to 8in
Armoured bulkheads aft:	10in and 4in
Main barbettes:	15in to 12in
Main turrets:	16in front, 11in sides, 9in back, 7¼in roof
Secondary barbettes:	1in high tensile steel
Secondary turrets:	1½in front, 1in elsewhere high tensile steel
Conning tower:	12in front, 14in sides, 10in back, 6 ½in roof, 4in floor
Conning tower tube:	9in
Conning tower hood:	5in and 3in
Funnel uptakes:	8in front, 9in sides, 7in rear
DCT towers:	2in front, 1in elsewhere high tensile steel

Horizontal Armour

Middle deck:	6¼in over magazines, 3¾in over machinery
Lower deck over steering gear:	4¼in

Displacement ***Nelson*:**

Standard:	33,313 tons
Extra Deep:	38,400 tons
Extra Deep:	41,250 tons with torpedo protection filled

***Rodney*:**

Standard:	33,730 tons
Extra Deep:	38,400 tons
Extra Deep:	41,250 tons with torpedo protection filled

Machinery

2 shafts with HP, LP, astern, and cruising turbines on each

8 Admiralty 3-drum small-tube boilers at 250psi

45,000shp for 23 knots at 160rpm

Speed	Shp	Rpm
10 knots	3650	64
12 knots	6250	75
14 knots	9900	88
16 knots	14,350	100
23 knots	45,000	160

Maximum Speed	23 knots
Bunkerage	3805 tons fuel oil
Range	5500 nautical miles at 23 knots 7000 nautical miles at 16 knots 14,500 nautical miles at 10 knots
Complement	1314 1361 as flagship

Career Highlights

THE YEARS OF PEACE

Nelson was fleet flagship from 1927 to 1940.

Nelson ran aground on the Hamilton shoal when leaving Portsmouth on 12 January 1934. There was no damage done and the ship was refloated on the next high tide, but the press had a field day with the Nelson-Hamilton connection.

Both ships attended the Jubilee Review at Spithead in July 1935 and Coronation Review in May 1937.

Rodney and the cruiser *Sheffield* were the first two ships in the navy to be fitted with radar.

1939

On 30 October *Nelson* was hit by three dud torpedoes fired by *U 56*.

On 29 November while on patrol in the Iceland-Faroes gap, one-third of *Rodney's* rudder was torn away by high seas. She was dry-docked for repairs at Liverpool.

On 4 December *Nelson* detonated a magnetic mine while entering the anchorage at Loch Ewe. The explosion was under the forecastle on the starboard side and the ship whipped two or three times. A hole 10ft by 6ft was torn in the starboard side and the side plating was dished in up to 4ft over a length of 70ft. A total of seven compartments were flooded and the double bottom fuel tanks leaked fuel into 'A' turret's magazine. There was minor damage all over the ship due to the whipping, but no fatalities. Full repairs in Portsmouth would take until August 1940.

1940

Rodney suffered a complete steering break-

Above: *Nelson* at anchor after her 1940 refit and repair showing good details of the external degaussing cable. Notice how the paint has weathered. *(By courtesy of Ray Bean)*

down when arriving at Greenock from patrol on 24 February.

On 9 April, while off the Norwegian port of Bergen, *Rodney* was hit by an 1100-pound bomb which hit the shelter deck just forward of the funnel. It penetrated the weather and main decks but broke up when it hit the 4in main armoured deck and only partially detonated. The forward 6in turret on the port side was put temporarily out of action but otherwise there was only minor splinter damage and 18 minor injuries. It was a good demonstration of the effectiveness of the armour protection.

In August *Rodney* had a brief refit at Rosyth and remained there to counter the threat of German invasion. *Nelson* joined *Rodney* at Rosyth on invasion watch in September.

Both ships returned to Scapa Flow in early November where *Rodney* was assigned as ocean escort to several convoys as protection against German surface raiders. On one voyage in December she encountered ferocious weather which caused extensive leaking and torn plates in the double bottom. She was dry-docked at Rosyth from 18 December to 13 January for hull repairs.

1941

Nelson participated in Operation 'Claymore', the commando raid on the Norwegian Lofoten Islands from 2 to 6 March. She was then assigned as ocean escort to convoy WS7, a troop convoy heading to the Middle East. *Nelson* sailed on 13 May from Capetown in company with the aircraft carrier *Eagle* for return to the UK.

On the night of 18 May the crew of the German raider *Atlantis* lying blacked-out and motionless south of St Helena were horrified to see *Nelson* and *Eagle* come over the southern horizon straight at them. *Eagle* passed so close that her wake was clearly visible. The two British ships did not see the raider.

Above: *Nelson* after her 1940 refit and repair engaged in a gunnery shoot. Note the UP mounts and the stripes on the mainmast and on the HACS directors on the AA platform. *(By courtesy of Ray Bean)*

In the Atlantic on 16 March, while responding to a distress call from the Danish ship *Chilean Reefer*, *Rodney* spotted the German battlecruiser *Gneisenau* close by the burning Danish ship. *Gneisenau* escaped into the gathering darkness, forcing *Rodney* to give up the chase but she did pick up the survivors of the Danish ship.

Suffering from boiler and machinery defects, *Rodney* staggered into Scapa Flow on 23 April with only one operating propeller shaft. She sailed from Greenock for Boston for refit on May 22.

THE *BISMARCK* EPISODE

On May 24 came the shattering news that the *Hood* had been blown up in battle off Iceland with the German battleship *Bismarck* and heavy cruiser *Prinz Eugen*. *Rodney* was ordered to steer a southwesterly intercept course for the German squadron, but contact with *Bismarck* was lost in the very early morning hours of 25 May. *Rodney* reversed course and headed for France.

Left: *Rodney* after her 1940 refit fitted with two 20mm mounts on 'B' turret. Note the counter-shading on the 16in gun barrels and the detail on the turret roof. *(By courtesy of Ray Bean)*

On the morning of 26 May when *Bismarck* was spotted by an RAF Catalina, *Rodney* was 135 miles astern. At 18:00 hours the battleship *King George V* came up from astern and they proceeded in company at 22 knots. *King George V* soon began to draw ahead, drawing the laconic signal from *Rodney* that 'Your 22 knots is a bit faster than our 22 knots'. Late in the day an air strike from the *Ark Royal* succeeded in torpedoing *Bismarck*, jamming her rudders and damaging her propellers, ensuring that she could no longer escape. The two British battleships would be able to engage at leisure in the morning.

The morning of May 27 broke with a Force 6 gale blowing from the NW generating a heavy swell. Approaching from the north at 08:43 the Air Defence Officer aboard *Rodney* spotted *Bismarck* at a range of 25,000yds steering directly at the British ships. Only the *Bismarck*'s forward gun turrets could bear and she could no longer manoeuvre to avoid being hit or to bring her after turrets into the fight.

At 08:47 *Rodney* opened fire with 'A' and 'B' turrets, range 23,500yds, scoring a hit with her second salvo. At 08:59 she registered two hits on *Bismarck*'s forecastle, disabling *Bismarck*'s fore turret. At 09:02 *Rodney* and *King George V* turned due south to bring *Bismarck* directly abeam. *Rodney* was recording straddles with every salvo and disabled *Bismarck*'s two after turrets. During this 'Run to the South', *Rodney* fired six torpedoes from her port side torpedo tube with no hits. Coming back to a northerly heading, from 09:36 until cease-fire at 10:14, she steered back and forth across *Bismarck*'s bows with the range down to 3000yds, hitting continuously with both 16in and 6in shells. Two more torpedoes were fired. *Bismarck* sank at 10:39.

Rodney received slight splinter damage which caused minor holes in the bridge structure, a cut searchlight control lead, slight damage to the CPO's mess, and a wrecked telescope in the HA director. Her self-inflicted blast damage was considerable. The upper deck was depressed to varying degrees around the main turrets, with wood decking lifted and torn out. Deck fittings, skylights, breakwater, and railing stanchions were broken and distorted. Cast iron water mains broke and ruptured causing flooding in many compartments. The starboard torpedo tube door jammed twice and then froze solid. Deck pillars under girders were distorted and broken; some fore and aft girders were fractured. Partition bulkheads were distorted and split; ventilation trunking was split open and blown out.

Rodney resumed her interrupted trip to Boston arriving there on 12 June for a two-month refit.

In the mid-Atlantic on 4 June *Nelson* intercepted the German supply ship *Gonzenheim*, which scuttled herself after a brief chase.

Below: *Rodney* post-1942 refit showing reverse counter shading on the 16in guns and a boat on 'X' turret. This was probably taken en route to the Mediterranean for Operation Pedestal in August 1942 with *Nelson* steaming ahead of the aircraft carrier *Victorious*. *(By courtesy of Ray Bean)*

FORCE 'H'

In July 1941 *Nelson* was assigned to Gibraltar as flagship of Force 'H'. *Rodney* joined her on 24 September after completing post-refit trials off Bermuda. Both ships sailed that day for Operation 'Halberd', a Malta convoy mission in company with *Ark Royal* and *Prince of Wales*.

On 27 September an air attack developed with *Nelson* as the main target and at 13:25 she was hit by a torpedo forward on the port side. The damage inflicted was considerable as the hit was forward of the armoured citadel and the torpedo protection. A hole 30ft by 15ft was torn in the port side just forward of 'A' turret at platform deck level. The main hull frames and deck beams behind the hole were completely destroyed and some 3700 tons of water entered the ship, increasing her draught forward by 9ft. The main guns could still be used in an emergency, speed being kept down to 15 knots to reduce the strain on the damaged areas. There were no personnel casualties.

At 14:30 two Italian battleships, four cruisers, and sixteen destroyers were reported 75 miles ENE of the convoy and on an intercept course. *Prince of Wales* and *Rodney* were detached to engage the oncoming Italian force, *Prince of Wales* racing away at her top speed signalling for 28 knots. This was greeted with considerable amusement aboard the *Rodney* with her 22-knot top speed. *Rodney* and *Prince of Wales* were recalled when the Italian fleet turned away at 14:45.

Admiral Cunningham signalled to Admiral Somerville aboard the *Nelson*: 'Please accept a pat on the back to compensate for the smack in the belly with a wet fish' to which Somerville replied 'Thank you, but a kick below the belt doesn't mean much at my age.'

Nelson returned to Rosyth on 16 October. She would be out of action for five months.

1942

Rodney underwent a three-month refit at Cammell Laird beginning on 17 February.

Both ships participated as close escort for Malta convoy Operation 'Pedestal' in August. The convoy and escort came under heavy air attack on 12 August as it approached the Sicilian Narrows. *Rodney* used her 16in guns in barrage fire against incoming torpedo bombers and was hit by a bomb on the top of 'X' turret that bounced over the side without exploding. Suffering from more boiler problems, *Rodney* was detached for Gibraltar. A refit at Rosyth would last until 19 September.

Rodney was at Loch Cairnbawn on the remote northwest coast of Scotland from 23 to 28 September, where she was used as a practice target for an upcoming midget submarine attack on the German battleship *Tirpitz*.

Rodney carried out four bombardments of Fort-du-Stanton at Oran on 8 and 10 November during Operation 'Torch'. The shoot on 10 November from 34,000yds placed all the shells within 100yds of the fort, showing the great accuracy required to avoid hitting adjacent civilian areas and advancing friendly troops.

1943

Rodney was at Plymouth for two weeks in May to repair leaks in the tiller flat.

On 31 August both ships bombarded the Reggio area at the 'toe' of Italy to cover the Allied invasion across the Straits of Messina. It was judged a great success, with *Rodney* scoring a direct hit on an ammunition dump with appropriately spectacular results.

On 9 and 10 September as part of Force 'H' both ships were on patrol in the Tyrrhenian Sea as Support Force for Operation 'Avalanche', the invasion of Italy at Salerno. The force was under heavy air attack for the two days; this time it was *Nelson* using her 16in guns in barrage mode to deter torpedo bombers. On 12 September Force 'H' returned to Malta where the surrendered Italian fleet was now riding at anchor. The Italian surrender documents were signed aboard *Nelson* during a ceremony on 29 September.

Both ships sailed for home on 29 October, *Rodney* suffering more steering problems on the voyage. *Nelson* returned directly to Rosyth on 7 November for refit while *Rodney* returned to Greenock where her mechanical state was assessed and found to be 'poor'.

1944

Rodney was declared 'unseaworthy' on 11 January due to severe hull leaks. This sad state of affairs led to a minimal refit at Rosyth from 18 January to 31 March where only work deemed necessary to keep her afloat was carried out.

Above: *Nelson* in late 1942 or early 1943 sporting her new camouflage scheme and three single 20mm on 'X' turret. Note how the crane boom lies flat on the deck when not in use. *(By courtesy of Ray Bean)*

Both ships participated in Operation 'Overlord'. Off Juno Beach on 7 June *Rodney* carried out a shoot against the 12th SS Panzer division, firing 132 16in shells. On the following day it was another bombardment of the 12th SS Panzer and on 9 June she took on the Houlgate battery and more German troop concentrations in the Caen region.

From 11 to 17 June *Nelson* bombarded the Houlgate battery and troop concentrations at Noyers and Le Havre. On 18 June she detonated two acoustic ground mines. One of the mines exploded 50yds off the starboard beam abreast the bridge; the other went off forward under the hull. The outer bottom plating was corrugated from 'A' turret to the fore end of the forward engine room, several double bottom tanks were flooded and there were leaks in the double bottom fuel tanks. Major flooding was limited to one compartment forward of 'A' turret, with slow flooding in others. There was extensive but minor shock damage to electrical equipment and the gun directors. There was no damage to the armament or to the machinery and there were no personnel casualties.

Below: *Nelson* on 4 July 1944: at this point she carried a total of forty single 20mm mounts, three of which can be seen on 'X' turret. There are a lot more life rafts in evidence but she is still carrying a large complement of boats. The new gallery deck can be seen behind the bridge tower. This also gives a good view of the distinctive shielding of the 4.7in mounts. *(US National Archives via Roger Torgeson)*

Right: A great detail shot of *Rodney* some time in the second half of the war looking forward as the middle gun of 'X' turret fires. It gives a good view of the shields on the 4.7in mounts, the end of the boat derrick, and the back of the bridge with the pom-pom directors fitted in the former 0.5in positions. *(By courtesy of Ray Bean)*

The mines were later calculated to have contained 1500-pound charges, twice what the ship had been designed to resist. It is a testament to the nature of her defensive systems that damage was so limited. Just four days later she was bound for Philadelphia for complete repairs to her hull that would take the rest of the year.

Rodney resumed bombardment operations on 26 June. The most effective was a controlled shoot 17 miles inland from Gold Beach which left the German survivors in a state of shock. The effect of 2000-pound shells landing with great accuracy every few seconds is something best read about, not experienced! By the time she left the gun line on 9 July she had carried out seven major bombardments, firing 519 16in shells, leaving devastation and chaos in her wake. It was the most sustained and successful operation of the war for either of the sisters.

A shoot was carried out on August 12 against Blücher battery on the Channel Island of Alderney. Seventy-five 16in shells were placed in the vicinity of the target.

On 16 September she sailed as part of the escort for Russian convoy JW60 on her last operational trip of the war.

1945

Rodney remained at Scapa Flow as Home Fleet flagship until May 1945. On 30 November she paid off into reserve.

Nelson finished refit in Philadelphia on 14 January and was assigned to the Eastern Fleet. On 19 July she sailed from Trincomalee on her last mission of the war, Operation 'Livery', covering a minesweeping effort off the Malaysian island of Phuket. She was at Trincomalee when VJ-Day was celebrated on 15 August.

At Penang on 3 September senior Japanese officers came aboard to formally surrender all troops in the area, the surrender document being signed at the same table used for the Italian surrender in 1943. She then sailed for Singapore where she was present at the surrender of all Japanese forces in SE Asia on 12 September. She arrived at Portsmouth on 17 November to relieve *Rodney* as Home Fleet flagship.

POST-WAR

Rodney remained in reserve at Rosyth until March 1948 when she was transferred to the disposal list.

Nelson remained as part of the active fleet until April 1946 when she was transferred to the training squadron. *Nelson* was placed in reserve in October 1947 and allocated for disposal in May 1948.

Rodney arrived at Inverkeithing for scrapping in March 1948. *Nelson* followed her there one year later, her final demolition taking place at Troon in December 1949.

Below: *Nelson* in the summer of 1945 in her final appearance. *(By courtesy of Ray Bean)*

Model Products

1:1200/1:1250 scale

The two battleships have been produced by many manufacturers over the years and many are still available, even if only intermittently or at 'swap meets'.

NAVIS NEPTUNE *RODNEY* & *NELSON* 1:1250 Scale

The well-known and prolific German manufacturer of white metal models Navis Neptun produces models of both vessels – part 1102 represents HMS *Rodney* as in 1942 and part 1102a represents HMS *Nelson* as in 1945. In the standard form, these are both painted light grey with a few black highlights but the company also produces a more detailed model which includes rigging and is mounted in a Perspex case on a wooden base.

Below: The Navis Neptun detailed model of HMS *Rodney* in a perspex case and including rigging.

Left, upper: The Navis Neptun model of HMS *Rodney* (1102).

Left, lower: The Navis Neptun model of HMS *Nelson* (1102a).

1:700 scale

TAMIYA *RODNEY* & *NELSON* 1:700 Scale

The well-known Japanese manufacturer Tamiya has released two individual kits, one for HMS *Rodney* and one for HMS *Nelson*. The first release (HMS *Nelson*) was in 1974 and the second (HMS *Rodney*) was released in 1977 but both kits are currently (2024) still available. These kits were part of the multi-company 'Water Line Series' and hence included a single-piece hull and deck with a separate waterline plate, the latter being moulded in black whilst the remainder of the kit was moulded in light grey. The waterline plate included the location for a sheet of metal supplied in the kit, which gave the completed model considerable weight.

The two kits contain similar but not identical mouldings, with the exception of the hull, although the instructions indicate that the hull should be different: for instance, showing additional location holes for AA weapons on the quarterdeck of HMS *Nelson*.

In addition to the hull and waterline plate, each kit contains two sprues. The sprue identified as Sprue 'A' is identical in each kit but Sprue 'B', which includes a nameplate, is different. These alternative sprues reflect the differences in armament, boat outfit and masts, as well as other small details and are very obvious.

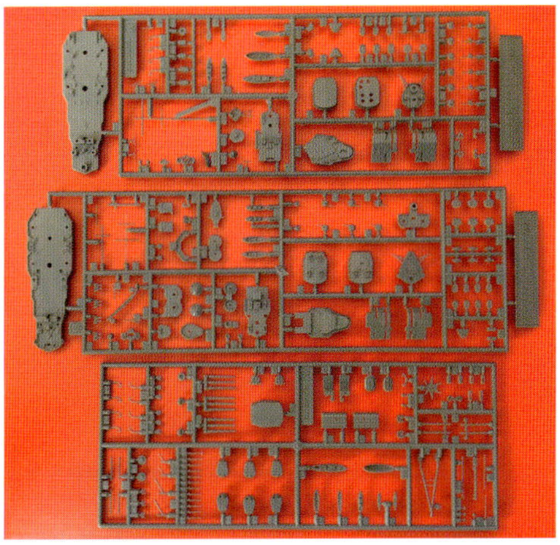

Left: At the top is sprue 'B' for HMS *Rodney* with that for HMS *Nelson* below and the common sprue 'A' at the bottom

Instructions are contained on a single, double-sided sheet. Side 1 gives details of the ship's history with technical parameters plus painting details. Plan and profile drawings of HMS *Nelson* show her as in 1945 with a simple dark grey hull panel with light grey elsewhere, and a profile only shows her as in 1943 when wearing a four-colour Admiralty camouflage scheme. No paint manufacturer is specified but paint mixtures are suggested, *eg* the deck is an equal mix of dark yellow and buff. The colours for the camouflage scheme are defined using the standard Admiralty codes. The plan and profile drawings for HMS *Rodney* show her in a light grey (pre-war) colour scheme whilst a profile only portrays her in a five-colour camouflage scheme as in 1944, the colours being specified in the same manner as for HMS *Nelson*. The profile does show other differences which are not reflected in the pictorial instructions on the other side of the sheet, nor are the alternative parts supplied as part of the kit.

The pictorial instructions begin with sub-assembles for the armament, mast and crane, moving to the bridge and superstructure before the final assembly. Picture 7 of the instructions for HMS *Nelson* does include the drilling of additional holes in the quarterdeck area, the precise locations being shown on the underside of the moulding. Reference to other sources is required to produce a truly accurate model of either ship at a particular date.

Although fifty years old, Tamiya were a pioneering company in high-quality moulding and hence these kits still match the standards shown by many more recent kits from other manufacturers.

Below: The boxes for the two kits from Tamiya both have interesting artworks on them

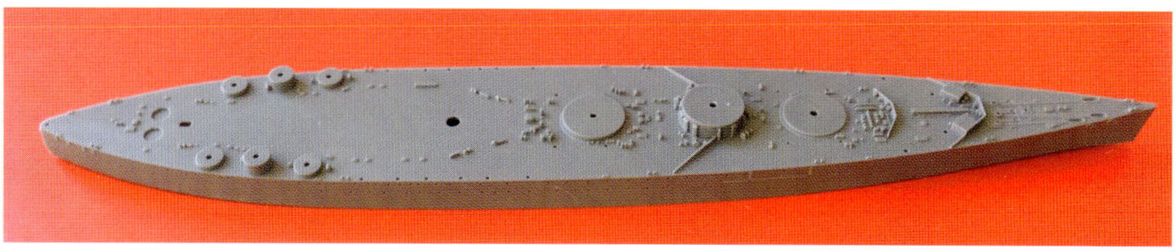

Right: The hull is common to both kits although the model of HMS *Nelson* does require some additional holes to be drilled in it

TRUMPETER *RODNEY* & *NELSON* — 1:700 Scale

The model of HMS *Nelson*, as in 1944, was released in 2018, as was that for HMS *Rodney*. It includes a simple camouflage pattern of a dark blue-grey rectangle on both sides of a light grey hull. The kits include a one-piece waterline hull with a separate deck. The three main superstructure/bridge mouldings are contained on one sprue, sprue 'D'. There are nine other sprues of five different types. The sprues are in plastic bags with foam wrapped round the very fine masts for additional protection.

There is a small photo-etch sheet

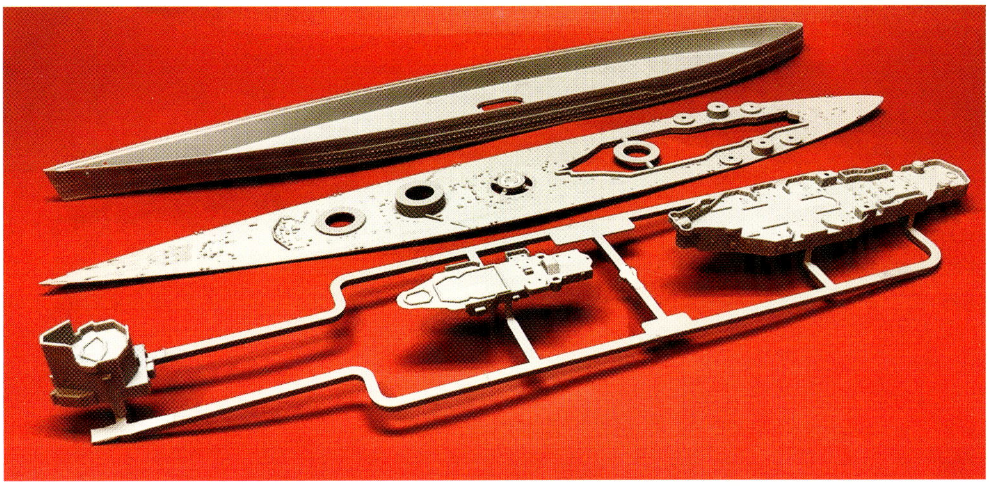

containing antennas, the funnel grille and the crane jib, but no guardrails. The decal sheet contains white ensigns and union jacks. Instructions are supplied in a twelve-page illustrated booklet, with a separate coloured painting guide. The eight colours listed are all available from Mr Hobby, Vallejo and Humbrol, and there is a large nameplate for display purposes.

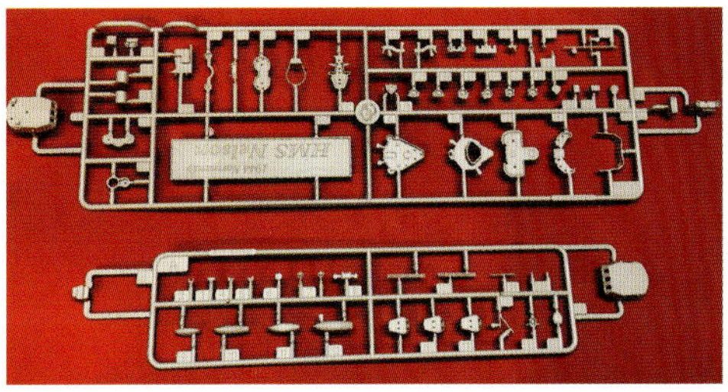

MENG *RODNEY* — 1:700 Scale

The Chinese (Hong Kong) company Meng have aimed this model at newcomers to the hobby, particularly youngsters. As such, the kit clips together (although the odd drop of adhesive will not come amiss) and the plastic is pre-coloured, although the grey, and particularly the brown deck plastic, are rather dark. The kit includes a dark red underwater hull, a black waterline, a grey hull and deck and a brown 'wooden' overlay.

Assembly instructions are provided on a large, double-sided sheet, containing 18

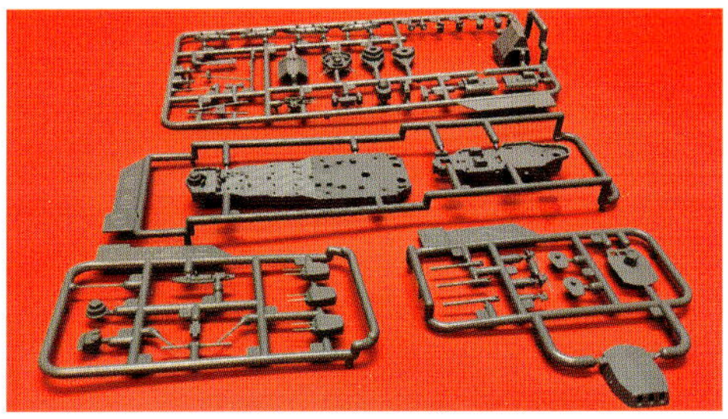

assembly diagrams. There is a second large sheet containing background details of the battleship, mainly in Chinese, but with parts translated. This sheet does also include a painting diagram, quoting paints from the AK Interactive range. There are 10 sprues of details.

If painted, this kit can produce a quality model without the modeller needing a high level of skill.

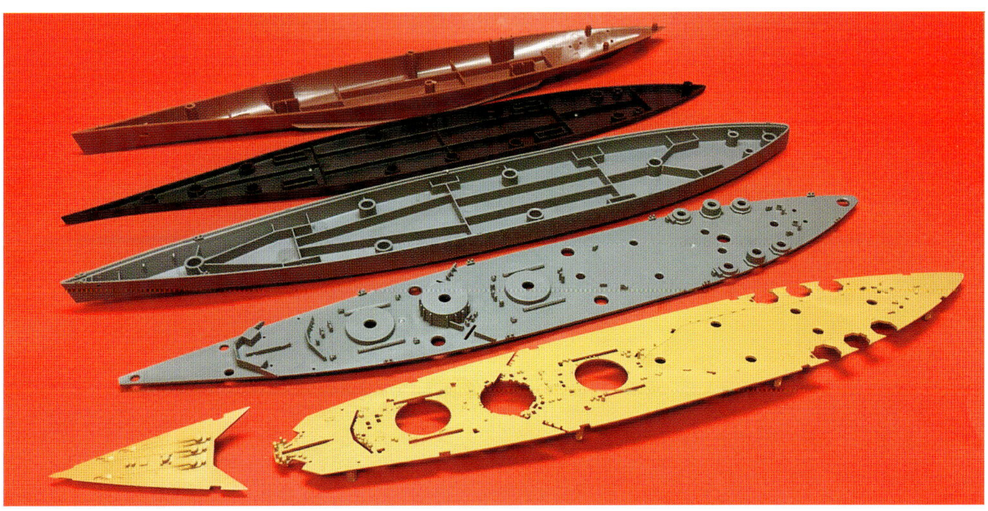

1:600 scale

AIRFIX *NELSON* 1:600 Scale

The British company Airfix is also well known as a pioneer of plastic kits but the company's main reputation is for supplying 'pocket money' kits rather than high-quality mouldings. The warship kits were produced at a scale of 1:600, or 50ft to the inch, and included a full-hull model, the hull being split along the centreline, with a separate deck. Only one kit was produced, for HMS *Nelson*, and this was released in 1961, becoming the seventh warship model from this manufacturer.

In addition to the hull, there are six sprues containing the superstructure, funnel, armament and boats. No indication is given as to the date the model represents but the kit does include six octuple 2pdr gun mountings, four quadruple 40mm Bofors gun mountings and six single 4.7in gun mountings, which suggest a relatively late date, although the colour scheme given in the instructions is just plain grey, with a wooden main deck and olive superstructure decks. There is an error in the painting diagram as it shows one of the octuple 2pdr gun mountings on top of 'B' turret in the profile (and in the assembly instructions) but on top of 'X' turret in the plan view.

The instructions begin with a history of the ship, in three languages (English, French and German) with the assembly instructions in pictorial format. The same three languages are also used in the instructions accompanying the painting details. A simple display base is provided for the full-hull model and many of the smaller details have a significant amount of 'flash' and moulding dimples on them. The model has been re-released a number of times and the level of these defects tends to increase with later issues.

Right: The box of the Airfix kit of HMS *Nelson*

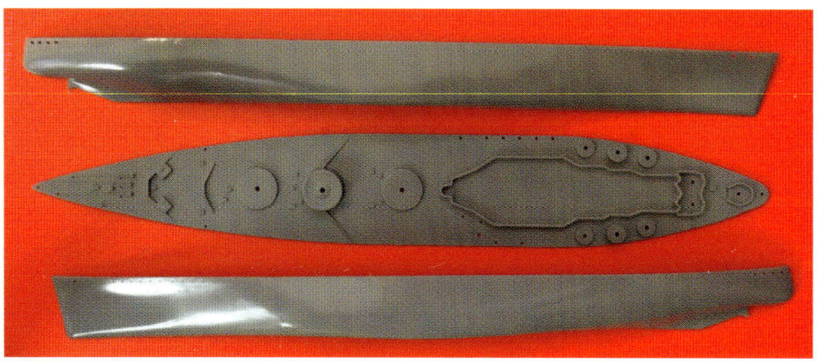

Below: The two halves of the hull and the deck from the Airfix kit

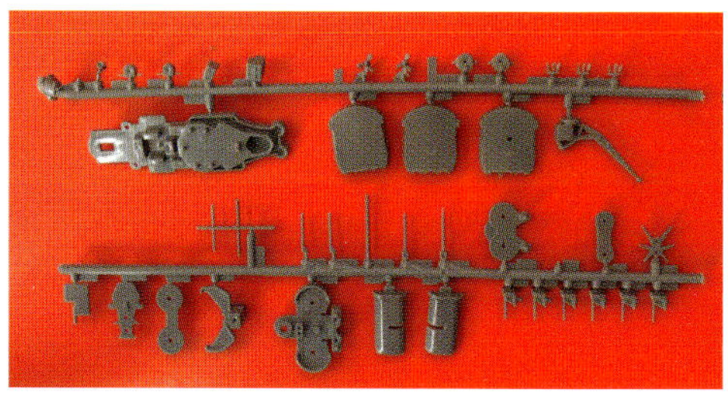

Right: The Airfix sprue containing the main turrets and other details appears rather 'scruffy' when compared to modern kits

1:350 scale

IRON SHIPWRIGHT *RODNEY* 1:350 Scale

The American company of Iron Shipwright released their 1:350 scale resin model in 1998 but it is no longer in production. Mastered by Jon Warneke, it includes a single-piece full-hull and represents HMS *Rodney* as in 1942, although alternative parts were provided to permit HMS *Nelson* to be modelled if desired. The kit comprised 150 resin parts and included an etched brass sheet.

Left: The resin hull from Iron Shipwright

Right: Some of the detail parts from the Iron Shipwright kit

TRUMPETER *NELSON* (1944) & *RODNEY* DRAGON MODELS *NELSON* 1:350 Scale

During 2024 both Trumpeter and Dragon Models announced the future release of kits at 1:350 scale, but at time of publication no further information has been forthcoming.

TRUMPETER ***NELSON*** & ***RODNEY*** 1:200 Scale

Inside the very large box are a one-piece full-hull moulding and four other boxes containing the '1300+' parts. Box 'D' contains the one-piece deck; the other boxes are labelled 'A', 'B' and 'C' but these letters do not relate to the sprue identifications used in the instructions. The sprues are all cleanly moulded and are supplied in plastic bags for protection. Both the kits for HMS *Nelson* and HMS *Rodney* include the same mouldings for the hull and deck but diagram 1 of the instructions details the different holes to be drilled in the deck for the particular vessel to be modelled, and diagram 11 details the removal of some scuttle 'eyebrows' near the stern that do not belong on HMS *Rodney*.

There are 40 pages of construction diagrams in an A4 landscape book, and an A3 colour diagram of the camouflage worn. A full set of paints is available from Mr Hobby and, where appropriate, alternatives are given from Vallejo, Model Master, Tamiya and Humbrol. The hull is stiffened by three full-height bulkheads before affixing the deck.These bulkheads are contained in box 'C', as are the larger components of the superstructure and the Walrus aircraft. Box 'B' contains the boats, cranes and the turrets for both the primary and secondary armament. Box 'A' contains the turret bases, gun barrels, AA armament, propellers and anchors, metal propeller shafts, anchor chain, ten small sheets of photo-etch (including railings and ladders), and a sheet of decals containing aircraft markings and white ensigns.

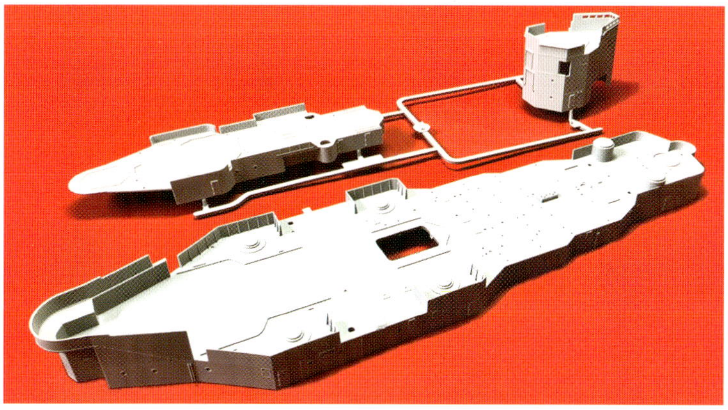

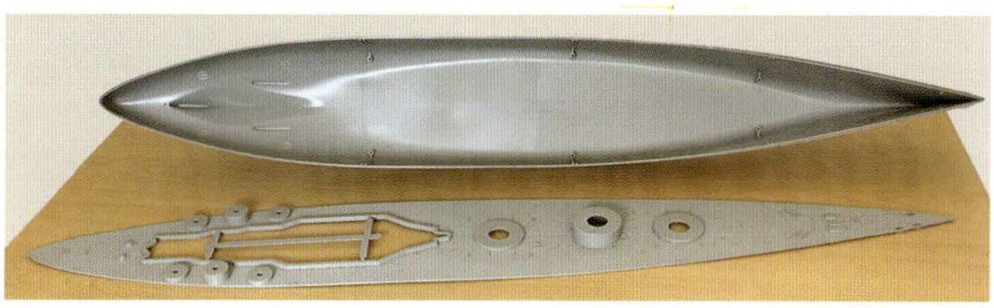

This is a magnificent kit, but not one for the faint-hearted!

Photo-Etch & Accessories

Etched brass, both at 1:700 scale for the Tamiya kits and 1:600 scale for the Airfix kit, is available from two companies – the American Tom's Modelworks and the ex-British (now American) White Ensign Models.

WHITE ENSIGN MODELS ***RODNEY/NELSON*** 1:700 & 1:600 Scales

White Ensign Models released their first sheet at 1:700 scale (PE723) in 1998 and their second 1:600 scale (PE629) sheet in 2001. The two sheets are similar but not identical, the majority of each sheet being taken up with railings and anti-aircraft armament. Both sheets include both two- and three-bar railings, those on the 1:700 scale sheet being plain but some of the three-bar variety on the 1:600 scale sheet include angled stanchions.

The anti-aircraft armament of both ships increased significantly during the war and so the etched brass sheets contain a variety of gun mountings to allow the modeller to make his (or her) particular model represent any time during the ships' careers. The mountings provided include single 20mm Oerlikon guns (48 at 1:700 scale and 60 at 1:600 scale), 8-barrelled pom-poms (4 at 1:700 scale and 6 at 1:600 scale), quad 40mm Bofors (4 at 1:600 scale only) and single 4in AA mountings (6 at each scale). A layout of AA guns for HMS *Nelson* is included on the instruction sheet but modellers are advised to check other references for precise quantities and locations.

The main differences between the two ships are provided in both scales – the bridge and the deck crane, with an aircraft catapult for use on models of HMS *Rodney* only. Other items, such as mast yards, ladders, anchor chain are included on both sheets but, whilst deck hatches are provided at both scales, doors are only provided at 1:700 scale.

Below: Top, the etched brass sheet from White Ensign Models at 1:700 scale with the equivalent sheet at 1:600 scale below

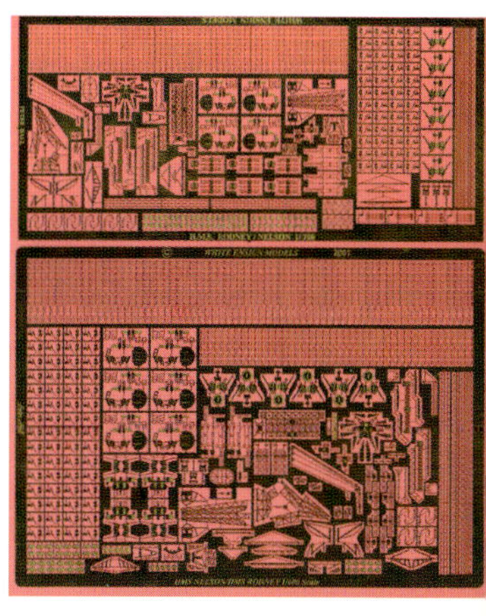

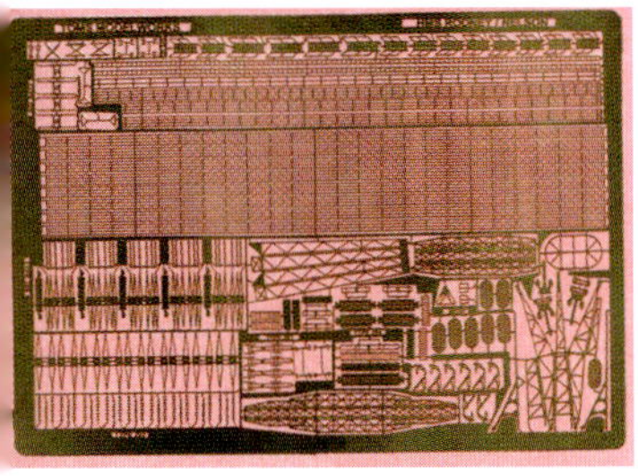

Above: The 1:600 scale etched brass sheet from Tom's Modelworks. The 1:700 scale sheet is identical both in contents and layout.

TOM'S MODELWORKS *RODNEY/NELSON*

1:700 & 1:600 Scales

The two sheets from Tom's Modelworks are identical in content and format. They contain lengths of railing, funnel grilles, davits, antennas, liferaft netting and anchors, which are applicable to both vessels. In addition they contain different 'aircraft handling crane booms' for HMS *Nelson* and HMS *Rodney* and the aircraft catapult for the latter. The instructions are briefer than those contained in the WEM sets, but do include a 'part' profile view indicating the precise location of the antennas.

SHIP YARD WORKS *NELSON* (S700006) 1:700 Scale

This Chinese company has produced an accessory set for the Trumpeter *Nelson* which comprises a self-adhesive wooden deck, six sheets of photo-etch, twenty-three brass gun barrels (three different calibres), and some anchor chain. Instructions are included in a 20-page colour booklet. As well as the usual ladders, railings and antennas, the etched brass sheets contain a large number of parts for 'facing' the superstructure, including decks and turret tops, and for constructing additional superstructure, lockers and other deck details. The instruction booklet requires detailed study to establish the precise location of these parts.

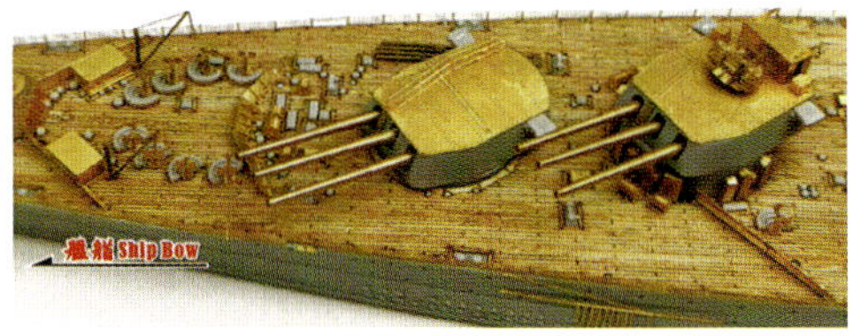

Right: Illustrations from the instruction booklet clearly show the extent of brass facings on the deck and super-structure.

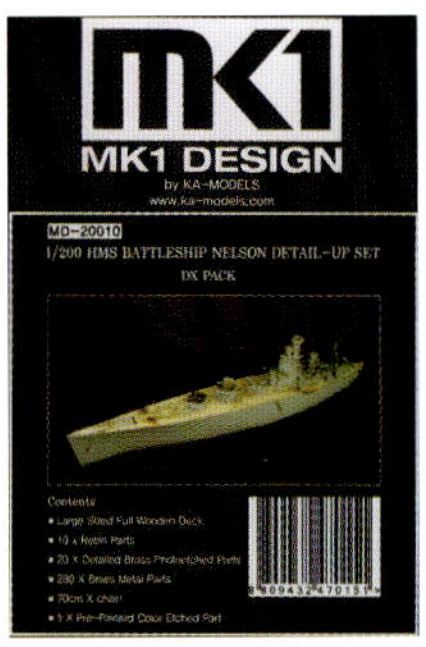

KA-MODELS & MK1 DESIGN *NELSON* 1:200 Scale

KA-Models from Korea produces an extensive detail set which includes smaller sets that are also available separately – Value Pack, Armament Set, and Mast & Radar Set. It includes a laser etched wooden deck, 20 photo-etch frets, 280 machined brass barrels and details, anchor chain, resin cable reels, and a pre-painted etched fret. The frets include details such as the barrel covers, flags, painted to simulate the pennants and flags for the flag locker and main gun turret top plates with the proper rivet detailing.

PONTOS MODEL.COM *NELSON* & *RODNEY*

1:200 Scale

Pontos Model of Korea produces two detail sets to accompany the Trumpeter kits, one for each vessel – *Nelson* 1945 and *Rodney* 1942. Both sets include 14 photo-etch sheets, a stained wooden deck, two brass screws (propellers) and a transfer sheet. The set for *Nelson* also includes 434 brass and 58 resin parts, whilst that for *Rodney* has just 380 brass and 34 resin parts.

There are 16 pages of illustrated instructions. The parts supplied include not only normal details, such as railings, boat and aircraft details, aerials, but the AA armament (20mm Oerlikons and 2pdr pom-poms) is made almost entirely from brass with a few resin parts. A great deal of research has been undertaken by the manufacturer to ensure the highest accuracy.

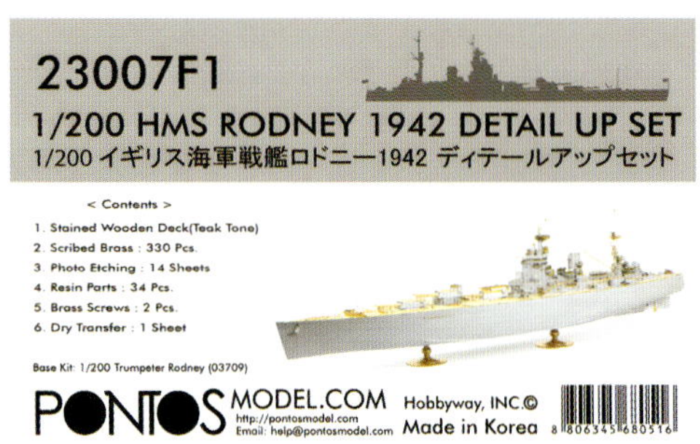

VERY FIRE TECHNOLOGY CO ***NELSON*** (VF700004)

1:700 Scale

This quite different accessory set, also from China, also contains an adhesive wood deck, anchor chain, brass gun barrels, but only four smaller sheets of photo-etch. It does, however, include some 3D-printed resin parts for the armament, and items such as platforms for AA guns. Instructions are provided on four sides of A4 paper.

Above: A similar Illustration from the Very Fire instructions shows the simplicity of the brass facings compared to those of the Ship Yard Works set.

ARTWOX, MK 1 DESIGN, WOOD HUNTER ***RODNEY/NELSON***

1:700 & 1:600 Scales

Wooden decks in 1:700 scale for the two Tamiya kits are produced by three companies: Artwox Model (China) (part AW20052 for HMS *Nelson*), Mk1 Design (Korea) (part MD-70020 for HMS *Nelson*) and Wood Hunter (part W7009 for HMS *Nelson*). Artwox also produce a deck at 1:600 scale for the Airfix kit (part AW50022). The construction of these three items is very similar – a thin layer of wood with planking with a backing layer of adhesive – but the approaches differ. The 1:600 scale offering from Artwox is in a single piece, as is the 1:700 scale product from Wood Hunter. Artwox have adopted a two-piece approach for their 1:700 scale product whilst Mk1 Design produce the deck in three pieces. Positioning and attaching the deck in several small parts will prove easier than just a single piece and modellers may consider cutting the larger items to assist construction.

As with all wooden decks, the first task is to compare the outline of the wooden deck with the plastic moulding. This is followed by checking the cut-outs, many of which will be missing with the others just needing pushing out with a sharp implement, and identifying any parts of the plastic which needs to be removed before attaching the decks. This will inevitably involve at least the anchor chains. Artwox and Wood Hunter include lengths of anchor chain to replace those removed from the plastic moulding, whereas Mk1 Design supply a small sheet of etched brass with anchor chain etchings. This sheet also includes the end supports for cable reels, as does the etched brass sheet provided by Wood Hunter; the latter also including etched fairleads.

Artwox provide a simple single sheet of instructions, which include details of the deck's construction, but Mk1 Design provide no instructions. Wood Hunter also include a simple sheet which indicates the locations of the six smaller fairleads but is less clear with the number and location of the larger fairleads. The instructions show just a general location for the cable reels. In both cases the cable reels provided are just the end frameworks which will need short lengths of plastic rod to complete them. Photographs will provide the precise locations for both the fairleads and the cable reels.

Below: Top, the Artwox 1:600 scale wooden deck with the equivalent 1:700 scale deck immediately below. Next is the 1:700 scale deck from Mk1 design with that from Wood Hunter at the bottom. These decks are all for HMS *Nelson* and 1:700 scale wooden decks are also available for HMS *Rodney*.

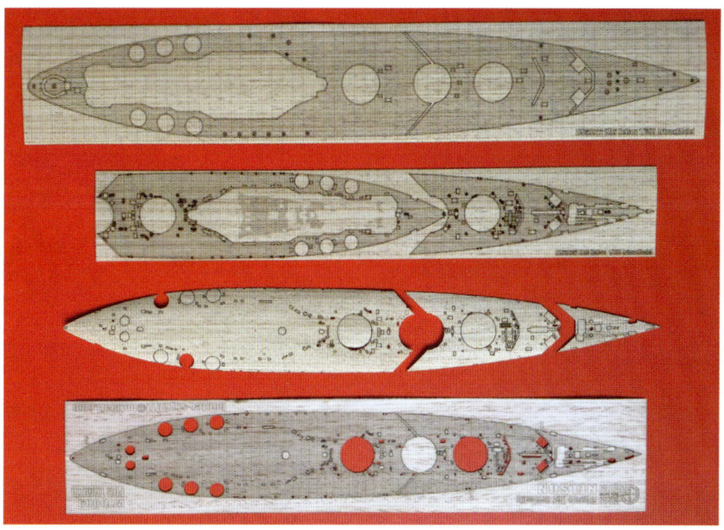

BRASS GUN BARRELS

1:700, 1:600 & 1:200 Scales

Turned brass barrels at 1:700 scale are available from two Polish companies: Aber and Master Model. Both companies produce nine barrels for the 16in guns (parts L-18 and SM-700-033 respectively) and twelve barrels for the 6in guns (parts L-19 and SM-700-034 respectively) but only Master Model produce six barrels for the 4.7in gun (part SM-700-035). The barrels from both companies are very similar, being hollow at the muzzle end with a spigot at the other.

At 1: 600 scale the 16in guns are available from B&D Barrels of the USA. RB Models (another Polish company) also produces a set of brass barrels at 1:200 scale. The set RBM200L12 comprises nine 16in, twelve 6in and six 4.7in barrels.

Below: The three different calibre barrels from Master Model

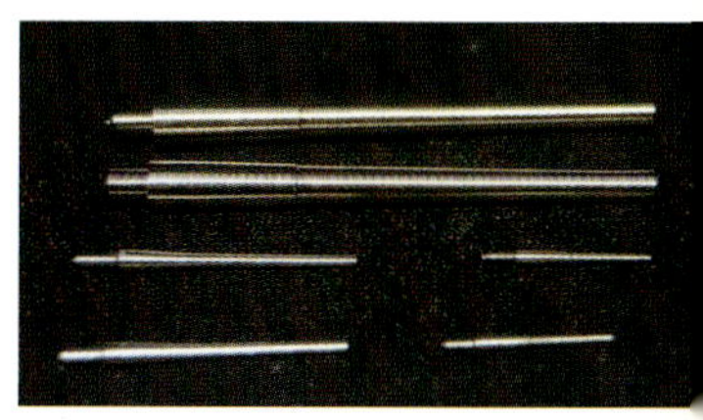

Modelmakers' Showcase

IRON SHIPWRIGHTS **HMS *RODNEY*** 1:350 scale

By JIM BAUMANN

HMS *Rodney* is a 1:350 scale Iron Shipwright kit, which Jim backdated to 1928 from the kit's Second World War fit. The plating detail is pencil shading and the open boats are from White Ensign Models shells with scratch-built interiors. Railings are also from WEM. Awning stanchions are scratch-built, as are the mast and forward director tower, and the accommodation ladder is adapted from a WEM photo-etched ladder. The sailing yacht is scratch-built. Figures are from Gold Medal Models.

TAMIYA **HMS *RODNEY*** 1:700 scale

By JAAP PLUIMGRAAF

This model, made from the Tamiya kit, represents HMS *Rodney* as she appeared in the late 1930s. Hull plating was created using a panel scriber. The fit of the kit was generally excellent although some of the 'after market' accessories needed a little attention to obtain a good fit. Etched brass from White Ensign Models and Flyhawk was used to detail the model, as were carley floats and boats from L'Arsenal. Rigging was made from stretched sprue. The ship was painted using WEM Colourcoats and Tamiya acrylics with Lifecolor acrylics for the sea base.

TRUMPETER HMS *NELSON* 1:200 scale

By OLIVER FLEURY

This is Oliver's first attempt at a model of a capital ship at such a large scale and it took him many months of concentrated work to complete the project. I think the images show that the result is credit to his dedication.

The images also show the amount of detail that is included in this large scale model, the wooden deck being particularly realistic.

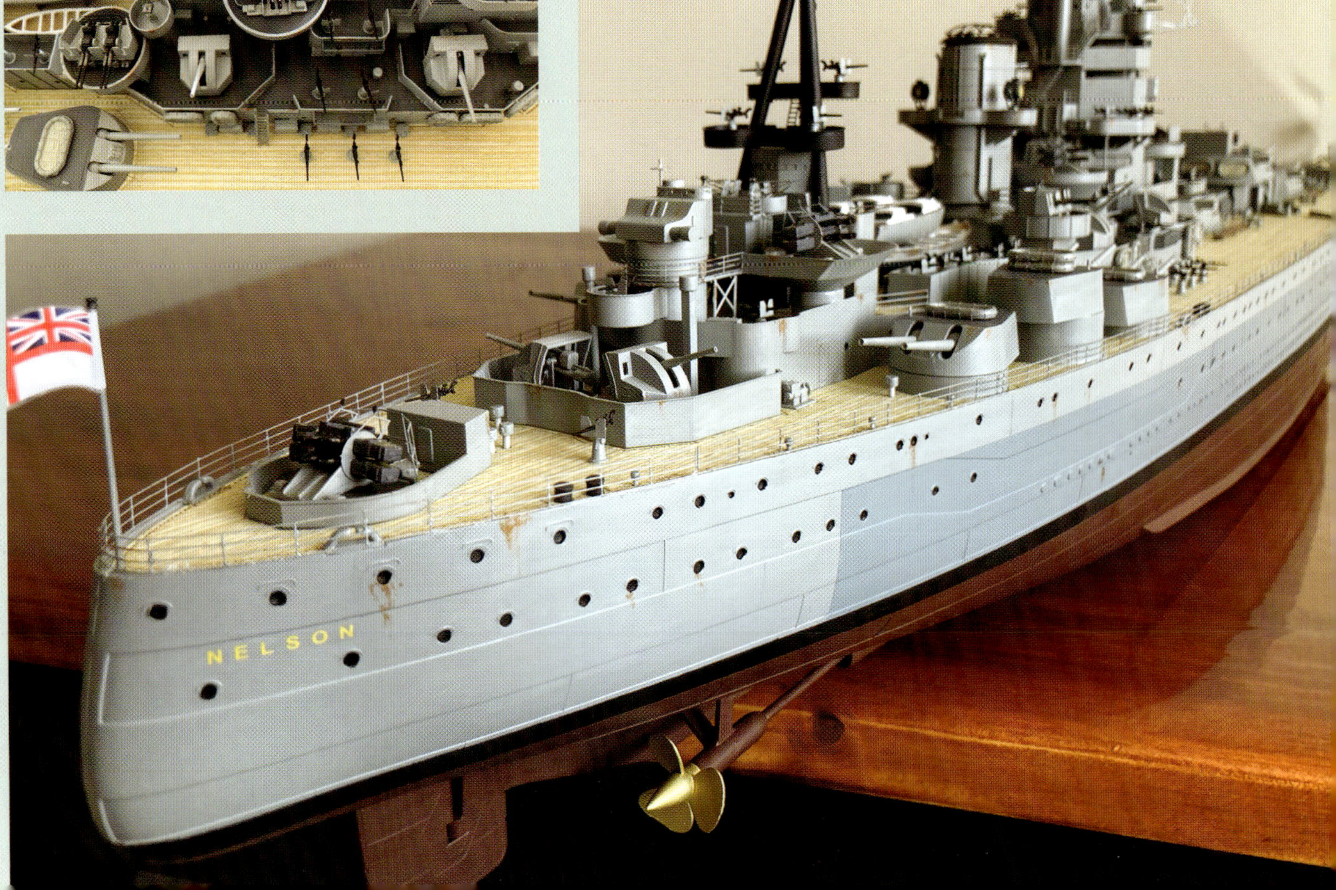
NELSON

TAMIYA **HMS *NELSON*** 1:700 scale

By CHRIS HEWITT

The model represents HMS *Nelson* as in 1946, by which time all ships were back to peacetime colours, although she retains the blue panel that she wore when serving with the Pacific Fleet. After researching the differences between the two ships, *Nelson* and *Rodney*, which Tamiya have taken into account in their models, the bridge, position of the crane, the single 4.7in guns (with shields on *Nelson* but not on *Rodney*), one

other main difference is that *Nelson* had a ladder system at the rear of the bridge where is nothing on the model, so this was all scratch-built, with spares and plastic card. The PE sets used are from White Ensign Models and Gold Medal Models. The majority of the photo-etching was superglued in place, but when it comes to the

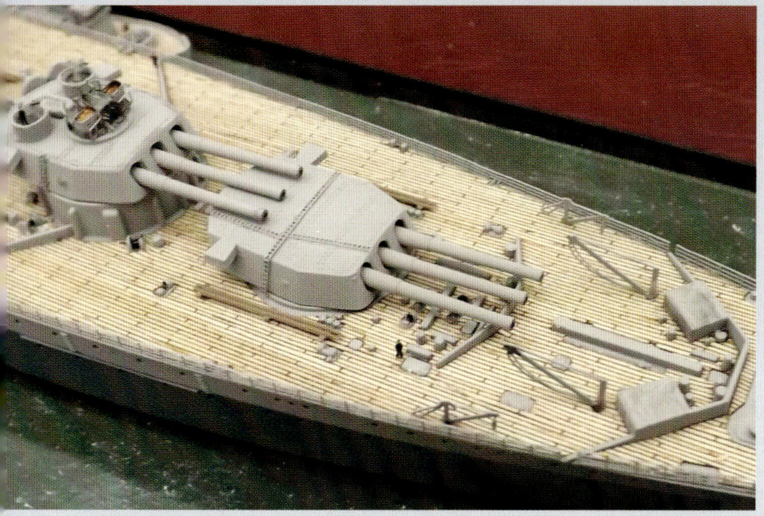

railings Chris applies any good wood glue as this gives enough time to fix the railings, fills the gap between the railing and deck and if incorrect can be pulled off easily and replaced. The wooden deck by Hunter was used as Chris thinks they really finish the ship off.

The 20mm anti-aircraft guns are from Niko but Chris didn't like the pom-poms on the WEM PE set. Crew figures are by Flyhawk, who have many different poses, including ones sweeping with brushes. The rigging is the UNI-can 20 den, which is very fine, attached using superglue. Brass barrels are by Master Model for the 16in and 6in. All the grey paintwork was sprayed and the rest painted with a brush.

AIRFIX **HMS *NELSON*** 1:600 scale

By REMY VITCHENIAN

The basic kit used for this model is the old Airfix 1:600 but only the hull and some basics parts of the model were used. All the rest is scratch-built. The photo-etch comes from the excellent White Ensign Models set. The LCT and the Churchill AVRE tanks are also scratch-built. The painting process uses enamel WEM and Humbrol colours plus some oil paints.

The ship is represented during D-Day, 6 June1944, preparing to open fire on the Normandy coast.

LCT 653

SCRATCH-BUILT **HMS *RODNEY*** 1:600 scale By PETER HALL

This model of HMS *Rodney* was built as a commission for an enthusiast in the North East of England. He wanted *Rodney* built as she appeared in her early camouflage scheme, around late 1941/early 1942, when the decks were still bare. There are plenty of photographs suggesting that *Rodney*'s decks were not fully camouflaged until later in 1943 when the main paint job was re-done, but soon after having the original camouflage painted on, the main deck was painted over in deck grey.

The model is scratch-built in 1:600 scale using some small parts from the Airfix *KGV* kit and the Walrus aircraft. The 16in and 6in gun barrels are from Steve Nuttall, and very nice they are too. The small details and AA mountings are from the White Ensign Models' *Rodney*/*Nelson* photo-etch set as are the Colourcoats paints used.

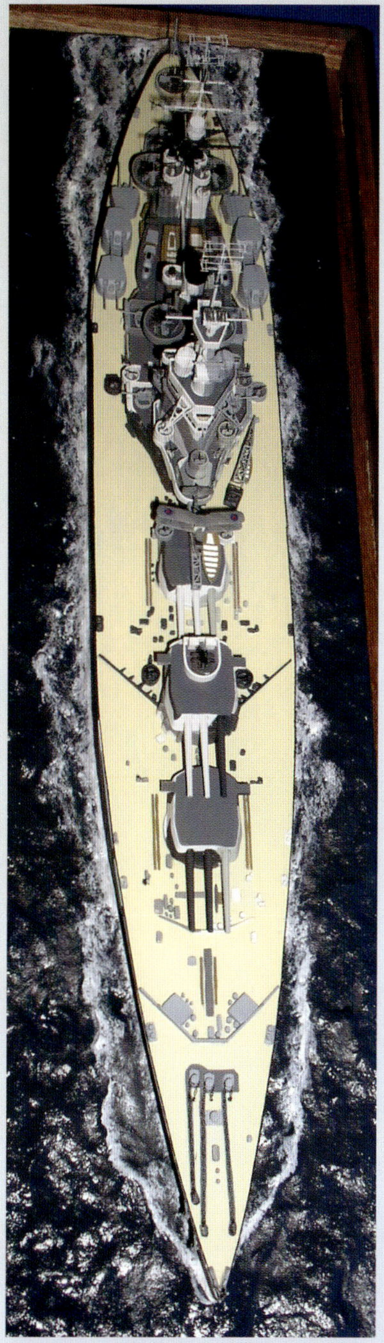

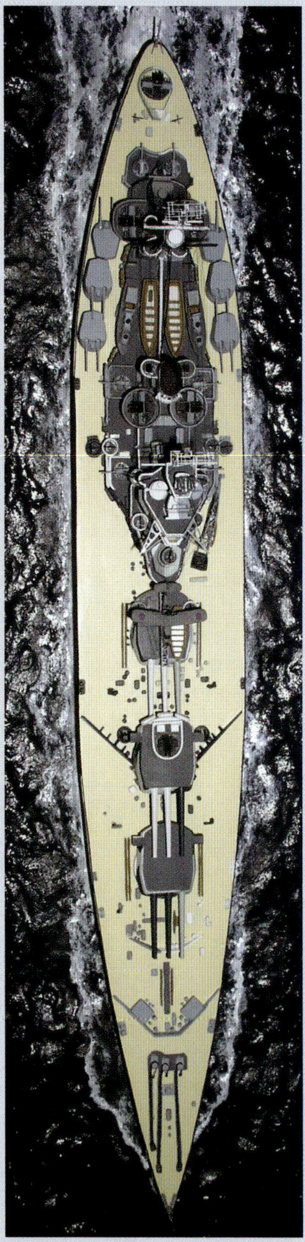

TAMIYA **HMS *RODNEY*** 1:700 scale

By RICHARD PRICE

This model was built from the Tamiya model of HMS *Rodney*, representing the ship as she appeared shortly after completion in 1927. It is a nice kit and the only significant modifications were the hollowing out of the upper bridge decks (adding new decks and housings), making a new main mast from brass rod and rebuilding the platforms at the base of the mast. Very little other work was required except to improve on the limitation of plastic moulding techniques by replacing various vents, cranes and other such small details. The ship's boats were hollowed out and detailed with

PE parts and scratch-built awnings. The dedicated PE sets from White Ensign Models and Tom's Modelworks were used to varying degrees. The main gun barrels are aftermarket turned brass; the secondary and AA gun barrels were handmade. Finally a few generic aftermarket parts such as bollards, cable reels and winches add to the overall 'busy-ness' of the decks. Paint is from the White Ensign Models Colourcoats range and the rigging is from fly-fishing tippet line, apart from the array between the funnel and the bridge, which is from fine copper wire.

TAMIYA **HMS *RODNEY*** 1:700 scale

By PETER FULGONEY

The Tamiya kit was first distributed in the late 1970s, and therefore needs some updating so Peter used photo-etch from both White Ensign Models and Gold Medal Models. Various illustrations were used to portray the 1928 fit, which includes cage aerials.

The weathering and shading is from AK Interactive and MIG powders. The rigging is produced using Ushi van der Rossen stretch extra fine, Caenis line, and Small Cars 0.1 wire. Each of these materials works differently and so have been used where appropriate. Caenis line threads through the plastic rig to make cage aerials nicely. The ring spreaders are made from 0.1 wire. This involves winding the wire around a needle, pushing them tight together and then pulling them away from the needle, and cutting them so that they fall off as rings. The rig is made from plasticard, and one of the rings is used to centre on the card so that five holes may be located around it. The number of spreaders is referenced from the illustrations, and marked off on the grid on the plasticard base. Three strands of Caenis are then threaded through the plasticard held at either end with bluetack. The ring spreaders are then glued into place with stationery gum. With the rings kept upright at all times, the last two threads can be located and glued. The aerials are then tied off at either end of the run with Caenis and the knot is glued with both ends of the strand being held in place by bluetack. When all is dry, cut off four strands of Caenis from either end of the rig leaving one strand to fix the aerial. Cut the securing knot around each end of the aerial. The whole line will droop but should be held together by the rings. Fit the whole piece in place on the ship. The wires may be tightened up by using the smoke of a joss stick. On *Rodney*, there are five of these lines with various numbers of spreaders.

Then, the Ushi line is used on long strands from fore to aft, and from the main mast trees to the starfish. Peter has sewn these on by fixing one end and then weaving the line round in and out of the crosstrees. Where the lines are short he used the Caenis, and for the funnel stays he used the 0.1 wire cut straight and fixed straight on.

There are a number of crew on board and to fix these Peter heated the feet of the crew over a candle until they glow orange, and stuck them straight on.

TRUMPETER **HMS *RODNEY*** 1:700 scale

By NIGEL DENCHFIELD

Nigel has completed his model to represent the vessel whilst she was participating as an escort for the Pedestal Convoy to the island of Malta in August 1942, the most obvious characteristic being the camouflage pattern which, as the images clearly show, was different on the two sides of the battleship.

HMS *Rodney* 1928

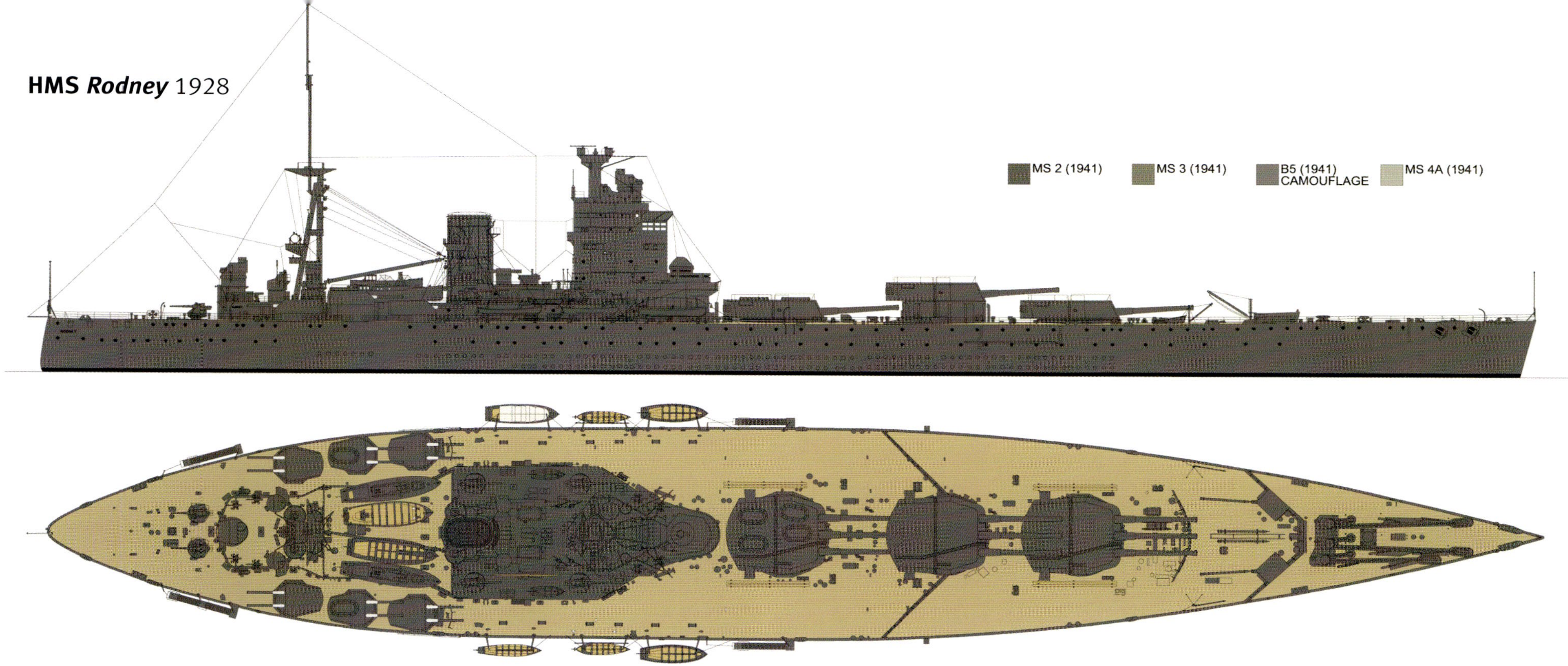

HMS *Rodney* 1940

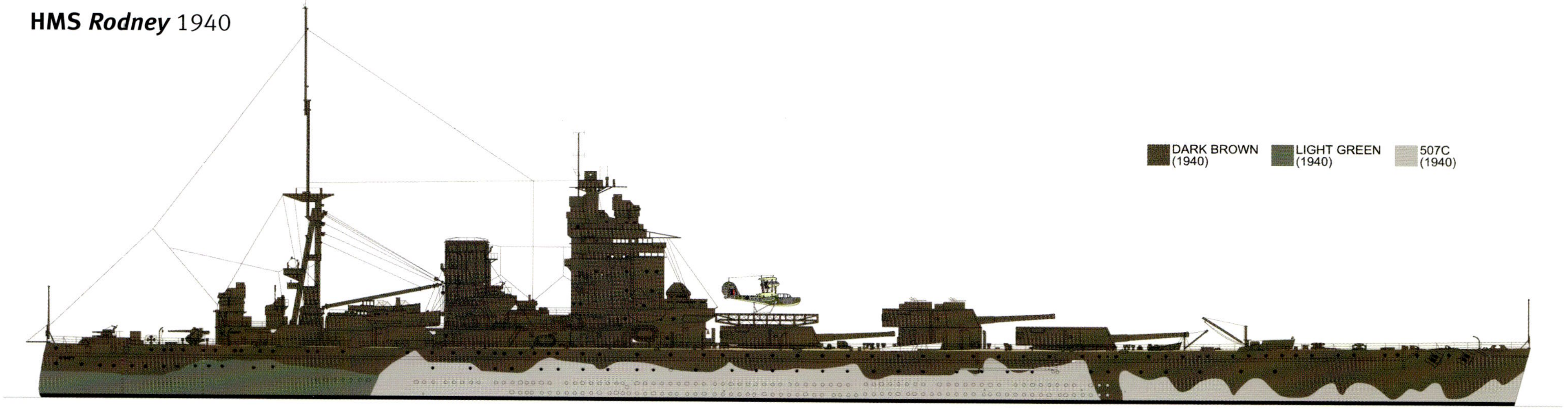

HMS *Nelson* 1942

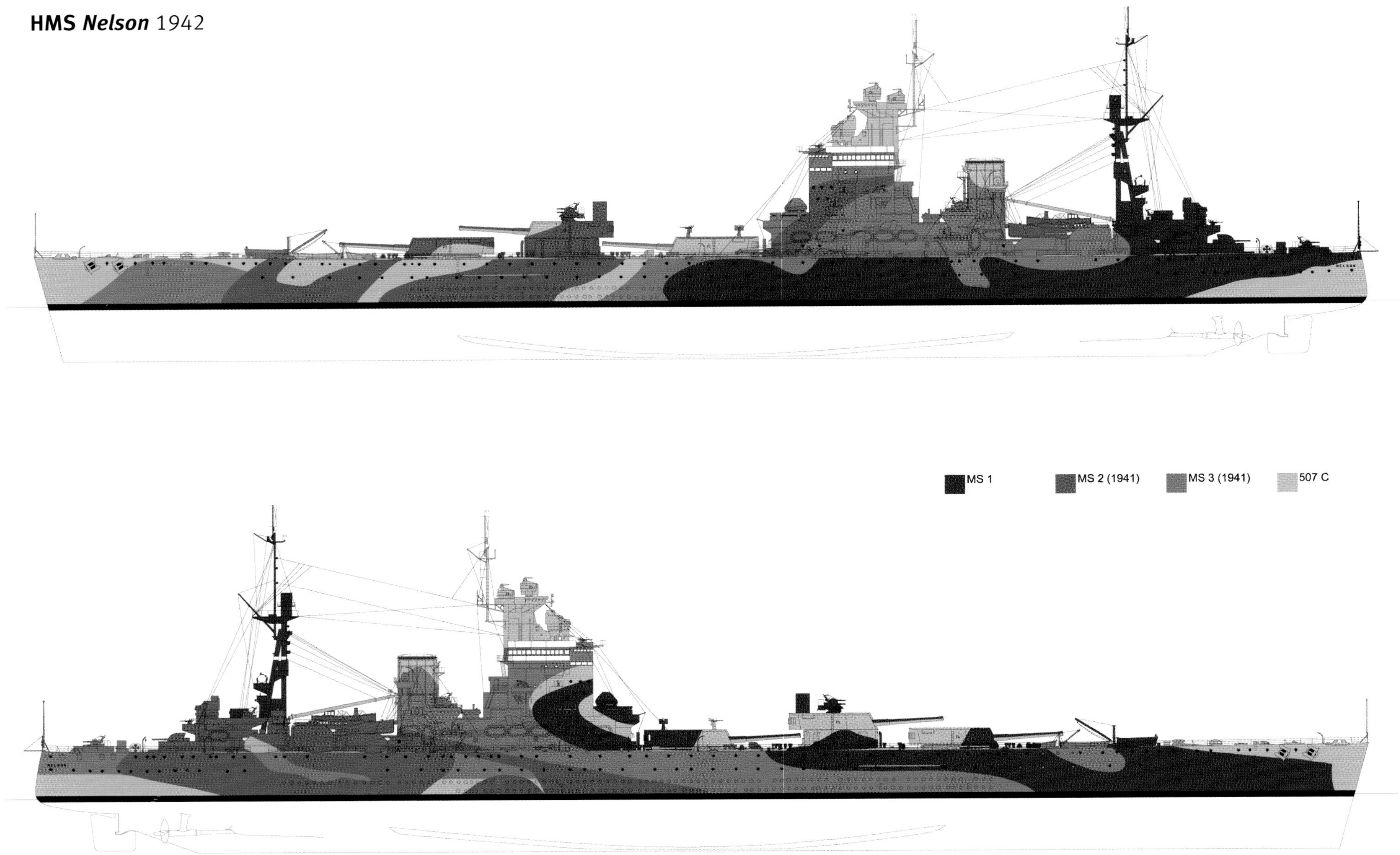

HMS *Rodney* 1942

MS 1 (1941)
MS 2 (1941)
B5 (1941)
507C (1940)

HMS *Rodney* 1943

MS 1 (1941)
MS 2 (1941)
B5 (1941)
507C (1940)

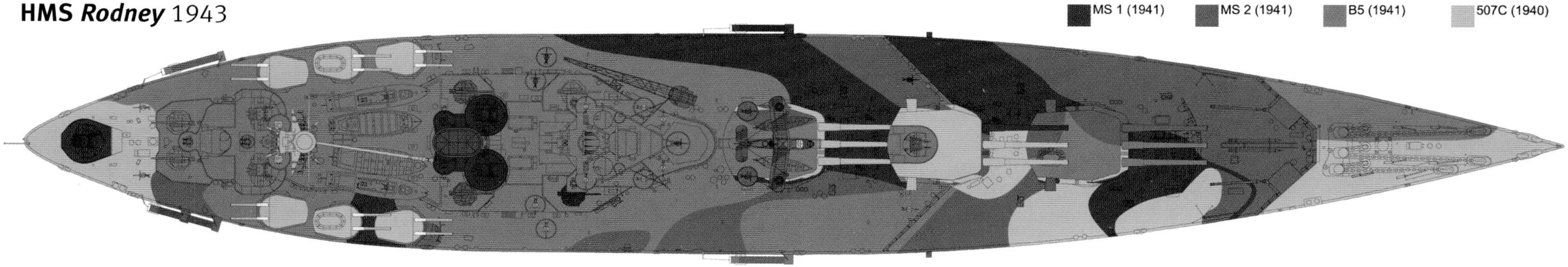

HMS *Nelson* 1943

HMS *Nelson* 1945

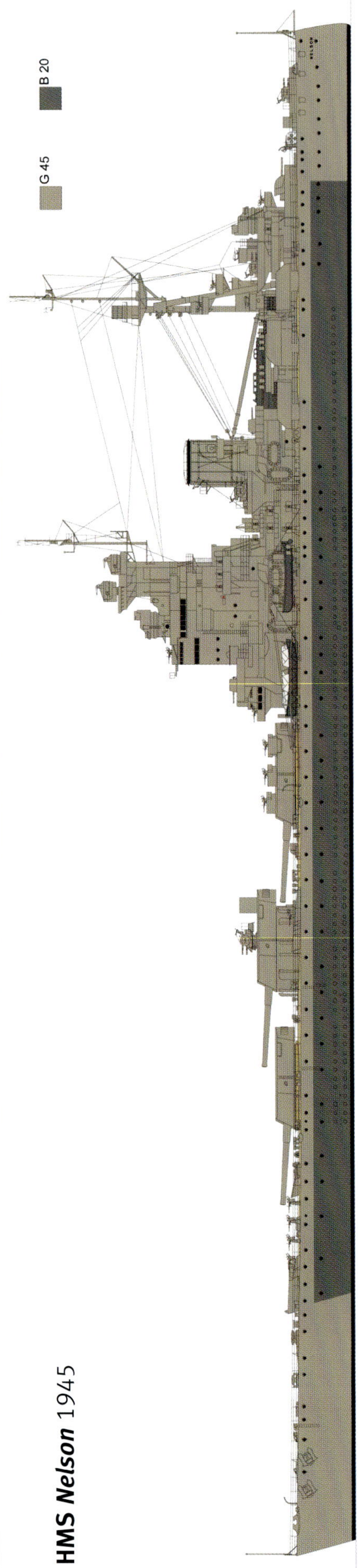

Appearance

Structure. The tower bridge structure consisted of seven decks. Starting at the shelter deck and going up, these were: shelter deck, conning tower platform, sounding machine platform, projector platform, captain's bridge and compass platform, admiral's bridge, and DCT platform. The AA defence platform was located at the top of the small tower on the DCT platform. The conning tower platform had a walkway that went around in front of the conning tower. Both ships completed with two rows of windows at the captain's bridge level. The 18in signalling lights were carried on the projector platform behind large concealing flaps. The main DCT for the 16in guns and two DCTs for the 6in armament were carried on the DCT platform.

The conning tower was immediately in front of the tower bridge structure. The top of the CT was at the conning tower platform level and it was topped by an armoured hood. The shelter deck was one level above the main or weather deck and carried the forward four 4.7in AA guns, the ship's boats and the mainmast. A second DCT for the 16in guns and two more DCTs for the 6in armament were carried at the aft end of this deck. Searchlights were fitted on mainmast platforms and on the funnel. The after two 4.7in guns were on the weather deck just aft of the shelter deck.

Pre-war alterations. On both ships, the upper row of bridge windows was plated over and the 18in signalling lights were removed. They also had the walkway on the conning tower platform extended aft on the starboard side to encompass a sponson, but no weapon was ever fitted there. Both ships had the torpedo rangefinder towers abreast the funnel replaced by octuple pom-poms by 1937, the work being spread out over five years due to financial considerations. The 36in searchlights were replaced by 44in models.

By 1932, *Rodney* had a 9ft rangefinder fitted to the back of the DCT platform. A triangular-shaped recess was cut into the bridge tower behind the starboard side sponson on the conning tower platform.

Nelson underwent a major change to her bridge tower in 1930 when a new enclosed compass platform was built at the admiral's bridge level, extending it out to the front of the tower. The DCT platform was later built out to the front of the bridge tower as well. She also had companionways fitted at the back of the bridge tower and extra deck armour fitted forward on the lower and platform decks.

Above: A close-up of *Nelson*'s bridge tower, taken during a transit of the Panama Canal in February 1931. Some recent modifications can be seen, including the upper row of bridge windows plated over, the admiral's bridge extended out to become flush with the front of the bridge tower, and the addition of blast deflectors under the after windows on the bridge that crew members are leaning out on. *(US National Archives)*

Left: An overall view of *Rodney* after her 1938 refit showing the catapult on 'X' turret covered in canvas. The lozenge-shaped extensions under the windows on the captain's bridge can be clearly seen. Radar has not yet been fitted and the Spanish Civil War neutrality stripes have been painted out. The triangular-shaped recess at the base of the bridge tower is an immediate recognition feature for *Rodney*. *(By courtesy of Ray Bean)*

Right: *Rodney* after her 1938 refit with Type 79Y radar aerials at the mastheads. This view also shows good details of the bridge blast deflectors, the wind deflector at the front of the admiral's bridge, and the extensions on the side of the bridge tower. The signalling projectors have been removed and their position plated over. *(By courtesy of Ray Bean)*

Far right: *Rodney* after her 1940 refit clearly showing the sponson and bridge cut-out (and just how the decks were kept clean). Great details of the blast deflectors and bridge extensions, as well as many deck fittings, can be seen in this view. *(By courtesy of Ray Bean)*

The original HA director on the AA platform was replaced by the new HACS Mk I on both ships in 1930, the platform itself being changed from a diamond to a more circular shape. *Nelson* had her HACS Mk I replaced by two HACS Mk III directors, which required enlarging the AA platform and widening its supporting tower.

Wartime alterations. Both ships were fitted with external degaussing cables, *Nelson* in January 1940 and *Rodney* most likely in December 1939. Both cables were replaced with internal cables, *Nelson* when under repair after being torpedoed in 1941 and *Rodney* in May 1942.

Other wartime alterations were mainly carried out to accommodate the increased AA weapon suite. Both ships landed the after 6in DCTs to make room for additional pom-poms. They also had a foremast added to the DCT platform to support radar aerials. *Nelson* had metal splinter protection added to the shelter deck amidships around the 4.7in mounts. The starboard side sponson on the conning tower platform was removed from both ships, but the triangular cut-out behind it on *Rodney* was retained.

Nelson's major refit in the US in 1945 saw the replacement of the armoured conning tower hood with a platform to support two quad 40mm mounts. Gallery decks were also added to the shelter deck and at the projector platform level on the bridge tower for 20mm mounts.

Below: A very clear view of *Nelson* after her 1940 refit and repair, showing the forward UP mount and the underside of the AA platform. *(Author's collection)*

Aircraft arrangements. *Nelson* was selected for aircraft trials in 1935 and was fitted with a crane on the port side of the weather deck abreast the bridge tower. The crane was retained when the trials were completed. *Nelson* was never fitted with a catapult.

In 1938 *Rodney* was fitted with a catapult on 'X' turret and a crane in the same position as *Nelson*'s. She initially carried a float-equipped Swordfish which was replaced with a Walrus amphibian prior to the outbreak of war. The catapult was removed in 1943.

Weapons. The 16in, 6in, and 4.7in armament remained the same throughout the service lives of both ships, changes being limited to the light AA weapons. The 4.7in mounts did receive splinter shields. The eight single 2pdr mountings fitted when built were removed from both ships in pre-war refits.

Both ships received multiple octuple (8-barrelled) pom-pom mounts. Two were placed abreast the funnel, replacing the torpedo rangefinder towers. One was fitted on the quarterdeck, and two were fitted aft on the shelter deck in place of the after 6in DCT towers. 'B' turret on both ships also was fitted with a pom-pom, *Rodney* being fitted with a quad mount, *Nelson* with an octuple mount.

Left: *Nelson* in January 1945 showing new upgrades received during her US refit. Most noticeable are the 40mm quads in front of the bridge, the 20mm mounts behind the forward breakwater and the Admiralty Standard camouflage scheme. The bridge wind deflector has not yet been fitted. There are two boats stored just abaft 'X' turret on the port side. The white areas on deck are snowdrifts. *(US National Archives via Roger Torgeson)*

Left: A superb view of the Walrus being hoisted aboard *Rodney*. Notice the 'bent angle' crane boom and the complete lack of any safety gear for the personnel working the lines. This is also a good view of the Type 79Y radar aerials. *(By courtesy of Ray Bean)*

Nelson was fitted with four UP (Unrotated Projectile) mounts, two each on 'B' and 'X' turret roofs. These were later removed. *Nelson* also later carried four Mk II quad 40mm mounts, two on top of the conning tower ahead of the bridge, and two aft on the shelter deck just abaft the funnel.

Both ships had 0.5in AA mounts fitted at the aft corners of the bridge tower at the projector platform level. These 0.5in mounts were removed and replaced by pom-pom directors. Starting in 1942, multiple single 20mm mounts were added

Left: An excellent view of *Rodney* after her 1942 refit, with a Walrus positioned on the catapult. Single 20mm mounts can be seen on 'X' turret in tubs, 2 on the conning tower platform, and one on the armoured CT hood. The captain appears to be addressing the crew. *(By courtesy of Ray Bean)*

Right: A view of *Rodney*'s forward 4.7in, in its original unshielded mount, after the fitting of the port side pom-pom in 1935. *(By courtesy of Ray Bean)*

to both ships. *Rodney* was fitted with 20mm twin mounts.

Sensors. *Rodney* received one of the first Type 79Y air warning sets in 1938. The aerials for this set were carried on the mainmast and on the foremast. The unit was actually meant for *Nelson*, but the aerial on the mainmast would have interfered with flying an Admiral's flag so the equipment was installed on *Rodney* instead.

Both ships received radar upgrades as they came in for refit and repair. Fits varied at different times, but eventually both had these sets installed:

- Type 273 surface search radar lantern fitted on mainmast starfish.
- Type 281 air warning fitted at top of mainmast and top of foremast.
- Type 282 close range AA fitted to pom-pom directors.
- Type 283 barrage AA for main armament fitted to barrage directors.
- Type 284 gunnery ranging fitted to forward DCT only.
- Type 285 long range AA fitted to HACS directors on AA platform.

Rodney had a Type 291 air warning set fitted above the Type 281 on the foremast and both ships had Type 650 missile jamming gear installed.

Camouflage and markings. Both ships completed in 507C light grey and alternated between that colour and 507A dark grey during the peace time years. Deck colours would have been dark grey for exposed metal and the turret tops, and the deck was

Right: Onboard view of *Rodney*, 1940, looking forward along the port side. All the ship's gun calibres are represented, from the 16in turrets forward, the twin 6in in the foreground, single 4.7in AA on the shelter deck, with an octuple 2pdr pom-pom mount on the platform above and the quad 0.5in on the bridge sponson; a newly added 20mm Oerlikon can be seen on the roof of 'B' turret. *(By courtesy of John Roberts)*

left its natural wood colour. The 6in turrets had linoleum on their tops. The mainmast was painted black from just above the searchlight platform to halfway up the mast above the starfish. Above this the mast was light grey. There were also white or light grey stripes painted on the mainmast and its supporting tripod legs just above the searchlight platform.

In 1937 both ships had Spanish Civil War neutrality stripes of red, white, and blue painted on 'B' turret. *Nelson* carried the letters 'NE' in white on the roof of 'X' turret from 1937 to the outbreak of war in 1939.

At the outbreak of war, both ships were in overall 507A dark grey. This colour alternated with 507B medium grey throughout the first years of war, both being in overall 507B at the time of the *Bismarck* action. It is possible that *Nelson* was painted overall dark brown in 1940. Counter-shading was applied to the 16in gun barrels with the barrel tops painted dark grey. In 1942 the counter-shading on *Rodney* was reversed with the barrel tops painted light grey. The wood decking was most likely painted over with dark grey.

Both received Admiralty disruptive schemes in 1942, *Rodney* carrying hers until she was scrapped. This scheme was carried onto the deck for a few months in mid-1943. Colours were 507C, B5, MS2, and MS1. *Nelson*'s colours were 507C, MS3, MS2, and MS1. *Nelson*'s disruptive pattern changed in mid-1943 with the MS2 panels at the bow being painted out with 507C. *Nelson*'s entire mainmast was painted black with this scheme, but the stripes were retained.

Nelson carried her disruptive pattern until her 1945 refit when it was painted out with an Admiralty Standard Scheme. Colours were B20 and G45. The top of the mainmast was painted in light grey. She reverted to overall light grey with a black mainmast in 1946.

Above: Looking aft from the rear of *Rodney*'s bridge in October 1940, with the funnel and its platforms prominent in the foreground. The two 8-barrelled 2pdr pom-poms have some splinter-protection added. Note the details of the pipework around the funnel. *(By courtesy of John Roberts)*

Left: An excellent view of *Rodney*'s bridge after her 1943 refit. Type 281 and 291 aerials are at the masthead, Type 284 gunnery radar is attached to the DCT, Type 285 radar is at the top of the HACS. Single 20mm mounts can be seen on 'X' turret, on the conning tower walkway, and on the conning tower hood. Seeing the number of men high up on the bridge tower without any apparent safety gear gives pause for thought, especially for the man up on the type 281 aerial way up the mast. *(By courtesy of John Roberts)*

Above: *Nelson* in 1945 showing the 20mm mounts and tubs on the roof of 'X' turret. Note the ready use lockers on both 'B' and 'X' turrets and the amount of stores under 'B' turret's overhang. *(Author's collection)*

Right: *Rodney*'s bridge tower from aft after 1935 with the 0.5in and port pom-pom fitted. *(By courtesy of Ray Bean)*

Identification features. When completed the two ships were difficult to tell apart. The top yardarm on *Rodney*'s mainmast was initially longer than *Nelson*'s, although it was shortened at some point. Throughout their service lives, they did carry their names in large letters right aft on both sides of the hull.

Starting with *Nelson's* bridge modification in 1930, the ships developed their own distinguishing features.

Nelson's bridge was made flush with the extension to the admiral's bridge and DCT platform, giving her two rows of windows on the front of the bridge tower structure. She was also the only one fitted with external companionways on the back of the bridge tower.

The admiral's bridge on *Rodney* remained set back from the front of the bridge tower and she only sported one row of bridge windows.

Rodney had prominent wind and blast deflectors fitted at the forward ends of the captain's and admiral's bridges. Both ships had the blast deflectors fitted to the sides of the bridge tower.

The triangular recess on the starboard side at the base of the bridge tower was unique to *Rodney* and she carried it until scrapped.

The crane boom on *Nelson* was straight; the boom on *Rodney* had the characteristic bent angle.

Rodney was the only one to carry a catapult.

Nelson was the only one fitted with UP mounts and quad 40mm mounts.

Nelson carried two HACS on the AA platform and its supporting tower was much wider than the one on *Rodney*. *Rodney* only had one HACS fitted.

Nelson carried the letters 'NE' on 'X' turret pre-war. The wartime camouflage schemes were unique to each ship and *Nelson* was the only one to wear an Admiralty Standard scheme.

Both ships carried their badges promi-

Right: *Rodney* after her 1942 refit, showing off the port side of her Admiralty Disruptive scheme. She still retains the catapult. The 0.5in mounts have been replaced with pom-pom directors. Note the large structure abaft the bottom of the bridge tower. *(By courtesy of Ray Bean)*

Left: *Rodney* post-May 1942 with 20mm amidships and on the conning tower. HACS Mk II with radar fitted and radar on main DCT. This is the starboard side of her Admiralty Disruptive scheme. *(By courtesy of Ray Bean)*

nently on the bridge face, and the 16in tompions on *Nelson* carried a bust of Admiral Nelson.

Proposed modernisation. A proposal was put forward in 1936 for modernising the two ships. The armour belt would have been deepened and more armour added forward to the lower decks. The 6in armament would have been removed and replaced with one of these three alternatives:

- Four 5.25in mounts per side, two additional pom-poms, and a catapult on 'X' turret.
- Three 5.25in mounts per side, two additional pom-poms, and a catapult on 'X' turret.
- Five 4.5in BD mounts per side, two additional pom-poms, and a through-deck catapult and hangar on the shelter deck. This would have resulted in a radical change to the superstructure similar to the rebuilt *Queen Elizabeth*s and *Renown*.

Nelson did receive the additional deck armour and *Rodney* was fitted with the catapult on 'X' turret, but none of the other work was ever carried out.

An extensive modernisation was planned for *Rodney* in 1943, but no work was ever done.

ALTERATIONS

When more than one 20mm mount is specified for a location, that number would be split equally with half the number on the port side and half on the starboard side. Precise locations for several of *Rodney*'s 20mm mounts are not known and are noted as **Probable** or **Unknown**

20mm mounts fitted in tubs are indicated with (T).

The minor changes to the Admiralty Disruptive patterns have been allocated to the refit periods closest to the time of the changes. This is for chronological convenience only; the changes may have been painted up outside of a refit period.

The removal dates of the external degaussing cables are based on a close inspection of photographs.

NELSON

As built 1927
Structure:
2 rows of bridge windows at captain's bridge level.
Admiral's bridge set back from the front of the bridge tower.
Weapons:
8 2pdr single mounts fitted, 4 on CT platform forward of the bridge, 4 aft on shelter deck.

1930
Structure:
New HACS Mk I fitted to AA platform replacing the former HA director.
AA platform changed from diamond to circular shape.
New enclosed compass platform built at the admiral's bridge level which extended it out to the front of the bridge tower.
Upper row of captain's bridge windows plated over.
Blast deflectors fitted below the after windows on bridge tower.
Extensions fitted immediately below side windows on captain's bridge.

1933
Structure:
Companionways added to rear of bridge tower.

1934
Structure:
Starboard torpedo director tower removed.
Sponson added on the starboard side at the base of the bridge tower behind the conning tower.
Direction finder aerial added on the main topgallant masthead.
Mk I pom-pom directors fitted on the DCT platform.
Weapons:
Mk V octuple pom-pom fitted on the starboard side abreast the funnel in place of the torpedo director tower.
Single 2pdr AA removed.

1935
Structure:
Internal 18in signalling projectors removed from projector platform
Large office added to the rear of the DCT platform.
Aircraft arrangements:
Crane fitted on the port side of the weather deck abreast the bridge for aircraft trials. Crane is retained after the completion of the trials.
Weapons:
2 Mk I quad 0.5in mounts fitted at the after corners of the bridge tower at the projector platform level.

1936
Structure:
36in searchlights replaced with 44in.

1937
Structure:
DCT platform was extended forward and made flush with the front of the bridge tower.
Port torpedo director tower removed.

Continued overleaf:

Weapons:
Mk V octuple pom-pom fitted on the port side abreast the funnel in place of the torpedo director tower.
Shield temporarily fitted to the port forward 4.7in mount; removed by March 1938.
Camouflage and markings:
Letters 'NE' painted on roof of 'X' turret. Painted out by September 1939.
Red, white, and blue neutrality stripes applied to 'B' turret.

.6.1937 to .1.1938 at Portsmouth
Structure:
Steering gear was re-arranged to be less vulnerable to underwater explosions.
Fitted with extra deck armour: 2¾in and 3in on the lower deck forward; 4in on the platform deck forward; 4in bulkhead fitted from the hold to the platform deck.
HACS Mk I removed and 2 HACS Mk III fitted on the AA platform. The forward one was mounted higher than the after one.
The AA platform was enlarged to accommodate the new directors and the support from the DCT platform was widened.
A new outfit of ship's boats was provided.

14.12.1939 to 4.1.1940 at Loch Ewe
Structure:
External degaussing cable fitted.

8.1.1940 to 29.6.1940 Portsmouth and Greenock
Structure:
After secondary DCT towers removed.
Metal splinter protection added to the shelter deck amidships around and between the 4.7in guns.
Main topgallant removed.
Foremast fitted to AA platform.
DF aerial removed from mainmast and placed on foremast.
Weapons:
Mk V octuple pom-pom fitted on the quarterdeck.
2 Mk VI octuple pom-poms fitted at the rear of the shelter deck in place of the after secondary DCT towers.
4 UP mountings fitted, 2 on 'B' turret and 2 on 'X' turret. Each pair was fitted amidships, one behind the other.
4.7in mounts fitted with shields.
Sensors:
Type 279 air warning radar fitted to top of foremast and mainmast.
FM2 direction finder fitted to front of bridge.

22.4.1941 to 4.5.1941 at Durban
Structure:
Annual maintenance.

2.10.1941 to 20.4.1942 Gibraltar and Rosyth
Structure:
Sponson at the starboard base of the bridge tower removed.
2 original pom-pom directors replaced by Mk III directors.
3 additional pom-pom Mk III directors fitted, 2 on the mainmast and 1 at after end of shelter deck.
4 barrage directors fitted at after end of shelter deck around the mainmast.
Submarine lookout positions built on each side of the CT platform.
DF aerial removed from foremast.
External degaussing cable removed.
Front bridge window blast deflectors removed.
Torpedo tubes removed.
Weapons:
UP mountings removed.
13 20mm single mounts added:
- 2 at the after end of 'X' turret's roof. (T)
- 2 abaft the conning tower on the conning platform walkway.
- 2 abaft the 20mm mounts on the conning tower platform walkway.(T)
- 2 on the extensions at the projector platform level.
- 2 at the front of the DCT platform.
- 2 on the shelter deck between the forward 4.7in mounts. (T)
- 1 amidships at the aft end of the shelter deck above the after 4.7in mounts. (T)

Mk VI octuple pom-pom fitted on roof of 'B' turret.
Sensors:
Type 273 surface search radar 'lantern' fitted to mainmast starfish.
Type 282 close range AA radar fitted to pom-pom directors.
Type 283 main armament barrage radar fitted to barrage directors.
Type 284 main gunnery radar fitted to forward DCT only.
Type 285 long range AA radar fitted to each HACS.
Camouflage and markings:
Painted with Admiralty Disruptive scheme.

21.9.1942 to 16.10.1942 at Roysth
Structure:
Maintenance.
Weapons:
1 20mm single mount added for a total of 14:
- 1 amidships at the forward end of the roof of 'X' turret. (T)

31.5.1943 to 7.6.1943 at Plymouth
Structure:
Gallery deck built at the after end of the projector platform.
Weapons:
0.5in mounts removed.
26 20mm single mounts added for a total of 40. New layout:
- 4 on the weather deck behind the forward breakwater.
- 2 in the middle of 'X' turret's roof
- 1 amidships at the forward end of the roof of 'X' turret. (T)
- 2 at the after end of 'X' turret's roof. (T)
- 2 on the weather deck abaft 'X' turret.
- 2 abaft the conning tower on the conning platform walkway.
- 2 abaft the 20mm mounts on the conning tower platform walkway.(T)
- 2 on the extensions at the projector platform level.
- 4 on the DCT platform.
- 6 on the weather deck between the forward 4.7in mounts.
- 2 on the shelter deck between the forward 4.7in mounts. (T)
- 4 on the gallery deck at the after end of the projector platform.
- 2 at the after end of the shelter deck.
- 2 on the weather deck just abaft the after 6in turret.
- 1 amidships at the aft end of the shelter deck above the after 4.7in mounts. (T)
- 2 on the quarterdeck between the after 4.7in mounts and the pom-pom.

Camouflage and markings:
Pattern changed slightly. MS3 panels on the hull painted over with 507C. Some MS2 panels painted over with MS3.

7.11.1943 to 2.12.1943 at Rosyth
Structure:
Maintenance.

2.4.1944 to 7.5.1944 at Rosyth
Structure:
16in guns relined.
Sensors:
Type 650 missile jamming gear fitted on the DCT platform abreast the foremast.

5.7.1944 to 13.1.1945 at Philadelphia and
1.2.1945 to 13.4.1945 at Portsmouth
Structure:
Turbines given a major overhaul.
Armoured director hood forward of the bridge tower removed.
Pom-pom directors removed.
4 Mk 51 directors fitted for quad 40mm.
Searchlights removed from mainmast.
Gallery deck added to both sides of the boat stowage.
Wind deflector added to front of captain's bridge (done at Portsmouth)
Weapons:
4 quad 40mm mounts Mk II (USN type) added:
- 2 in front of bridge atop the conning tower.
- 2 on the shelter deck just forward of the ship's boats.

21 20 mm single mounts added and others repositioned for a total of 61. New layout:
- 8 on the weather deck just behind the forward breakwater.
- 2 on the weather deck abaft 'X' turret.
- 6 on the roof of 'X' turret. (T)
- 2 forward of the conning tower. (T)
- 4 on the DCT platform.

6 on the gallery deck at the rear of the projector platform.
6 on the weather deck between the 4.7in mounts.
4 on the shelter deck between the 4.7in mounts. (T)
4 on the conning tower platform between the 4.7in mounts.
10 on the gallery deck abeam the boat deck.
4 on mainmast platforms.
2 at aft end of shelter deck. (T)
1 amidships at the aft end of the shelter deck above the after 4.7in mounts. (T)
2 on the quarterdeck between the after 4.7in mounts and the pom-pom.

Camouflage and markings:
Painted in Admiralty Standard Scheme.

RODNEY:

As built 1927
Structure:
2 rows of bridge windows captain's bridge level.
Admiral's bridge set back from the front of the bridge tower.
Weapons:
8 2pdr single mounts fitted, 4 on CT platform forward of the bridge, 4 aft on shelter deck.

1930
Structure:
New HACS Mk I fitted to AA platform replacing the former HA director.
AA platform changed from diamond to circular shape.

1931
Structure:
Upper row of captain's bridge windows is plated over.
Blast deflectors fitted below the windows on bridge tower.

1932
Structure:
9ft rangefinder fitted at the back of the DCT platform.
Starboard torpedo director tower removed.
Sponson added on the starboard side at the base of the bridge tower behind the conning tower. A triangular shaped recess was cut into the bridge tower behind it.
Weapons:
Mk V octuple pom-pom fitted on the starboard side abreast the funnel in place of the torpedo director tower.
Single 2pdr AA removed.

1934
Structure:
Mk I pom-pom directors were fitted on the DCT platform.

1935
Structure:
Port torpedo rangefinder tower removed.
Small rangefinder platform on the DCT platform extended slightly aft.
Weapons:
Mk V octuple pom-pom fitted on the port side abreast the funnel in place of the torpedo director tower.
2 Mk II quad 0.5in mounts fitted at the after corners of the bridge tower at the projector platform level.

1936
Structure:
An open compass platform built above the original enclosed one in front of the windows on the admiral's bridge.
Wind deflector fitted to front of admiral's bridge.
Internal 18in signalling projectors removed from projector platform.
36in searchlights replaced with 44in.

1937
Camouflage and markings:
Red, white, and blue neutrality stripes applied to 'B' turret.

.9.1938 to .11.1938
Structure:
Steering gear was re-arranged to be less vulnerable to underwater explosions.
Extensions fitted immediately below after windows on captain's bridge.
Main topgallant removed.
Foremast fitted to AA platform.
Aircraft Arrangements:
Catapult fitted on 'X' turret.
Crane fitted on the port side of the weather deck abreast the bridge.
Weapons:
Mk VI octuple pom-pom fitted on the quarterdeck.
Sensors:
Type 79Y air warning radar fitted at the tops of the mainmast and the foremast.

9.12.1939 to 29.12.1939 at Liverpool
Structure:
Repairs to rudder.
External degaussing cable fitted.

24.8.1940 to 10.9.1940 at Rosyth
Weapons:
2 20mm single mounts fitted amidships one behind the other on the roof of 'B' turret. (T)
Sensors:
Type 79Y air warning radar upgraded to Type 279.
Camouflage and markings:
Painted with unique green, brown, and 507C scheme

18.12.1940 to 13.1.1941 at Rosyth
Structure:
Repairs to storm damage and general hull stiffening.
Camouflage and markings:
Painted overall 507A or 507B

13.6.1941 to 11.8.1941 at Boston
Structure:
After secondary DCT towers removed.
Sponson at the starboard base of the bridge tower removed. The triangular recess behind it is retained.
Extensions fitted below after windows on captain's bridge removed.
Submarine lookout positions built on each side of the CT platform.
Weapons:
20mm single mounts removed from roof of 'B' turret.
2 Mk VI octuple pom-poms fitted at the rear of the shelter deck in place of the after secondary DCT towers.
Mk VII quad pom-pom fitted on roof of 'B' turret.
Sensors:
Type 271 surface search radar 'lantern' fitted to mainmast starfish.
Type 281 air warning radar fitted in place of Type 279.
Type 284 main gunnery radar fitted to forward DCT only.
FM2 direction finder fitted to front of bridge.

17.2.1942 to 3.5.1942 at Liverpool
Structure:
Hull, boiler and steering repairs.
16in guns relined.
0.5in platforms fitted with Mk III pom-pom directors.
3 Mk III pom-pom directors fitted aft, 2 on mainmast and 1 at aft end of shelter deck.
4 barrage directors fitted at after end of shelter deck around the mainmast.
HACS Mk III fitted on the AA platform.
AA director platform enlarged.
Heavier foremast fitted.
Large deckhouse fitted on shelter deck immediately abaft the bridge tower.
External degaussing cable removed.
Weapons:
0.5in mounts removed.
17 20mm single mounts added:
2 on the weather deck abreast 'B' turret behind the breakwater. (T)
2 at the after end of the roof of 'X' turret. (T)
1 on the roof of the armoured conning tower hood. (T)
2 beside the conning tower on the conning platform walkway.
2 abaft the conning tower on the conning platform walkway. (T)
2 at the after end of the DCT platform.
2 on the weather deck just behind the bridge tower. (T)
2 on the shelter deck between the 4.7in mounts. (T)
2 on the quarterdeck just forward of the pom-pom.

Continued overleaf:

Sensors:
Type 273 surface search radar 'lantern' fitted in place of Type 271.
Type 282 close range AA radar fitted to pom-pom directors.
Type 283 main armament barrage radar fitted to barrage directors.
Type 285 long range AA radar fitted to HACS.
Type 291 air warning radar fitted above Type 281.
Camouflage and markings:
Painted with Admiralty Disruptive scheme.

1.7.1942 to 16.7.1942 at Freetown
Structure:
Ship's engineering staff repair steering problems.

23.8.1942 to 19.9.1942 at Rosyth
Structure: Repairs to steering and boilers.
Weapons:
4 20mm single mounts added for a total of 21:
2 on the quarterdeck just aft of the 4.7in mounts, forward and outboard of the other pair. (**Probable**).
2 on the quarterdeck just above the pom-pom. (T) (**Probable**)

14.5.1943 to 31.5.1943 at Plymouth
Aircraft Arrangements:
Catapult removed
Weapons:
4.7in guns fitted with shields.
36 20mm single mounts added for a total of 57. New layout:
10 on the weather deck behind the forward breakwater.
2 on the weather deck abreast 'B' turret behind the breakwater. (T)
2 at the after end of the roof of 'B' turret. (T)
2 at the front end of the roof of 'X' turret (**Probable**)
2 at the after end of the roof of 'X' turret. (T)
4 on the weather deck abaft 'X' turret.
1 on the roof of the armoured conning tower hood. (T)
2 on the roof of the conning tower.
2 beside the conning tower on the conning platform walkway.
2 abaft the conning tower on the conning platform walkway. (T)
4 on the DCT platform.
2 on the weather deck just behind the bridge tower. (T)
2 on the shelter deck between the 4.7in mounts. (T)
6 on the weather deck, one in front of each 6in turret.
2 on the weather deck behind the after 6in turret.
2 on the roof of the after 6in turret.
2 at the aft end of the shelter deck.
1 atop the after DCT tower
2 on the quarterdeck just aft of the 4.7in mounts, forward and outboard of the other pair. (**Probable**)
1 amidships at the aft end of the shelter deck.
2 on the quarterdeck just forward of the pom-pom.
2 on the quarter deck just above the pom-pom. (T)
5 twin 20mm mounts added:
2 on the weather deck just below the second 4.7in mount. (T)
2 on the shelter deck abaft the single 20mm mount. (T)
1 on the starboard side of the roof of 'B' turret. (T)
Camouflage and markings:
Camouflage scheme carried on to weather deck.

6.11.1943 to 16.12.1943
Structure:
Plans drawn up for a full modernisation which was never carried out.
Camouflage and markings:
Camouflage scheme removed from weather deck.

18.1.1944 to 30.3.1944 at Rosyth
Structure: Leaks in the hull repaired. Torpedo tubes removed.
Weapons:
2 20mm single mounts added for a total of 59:
Positions unknown.
Sensors:
Type 650 missile jamming gear added, position not known.

30.8.1944 to 11.9.1944 at Plymouth
Structure: Urgent repairs. Possibly for blast damage caused by the 16in guns, recently in action off Normandy.

15.10.1944 to 26.10.1944 at Rosyth
Structure: Maintenance.

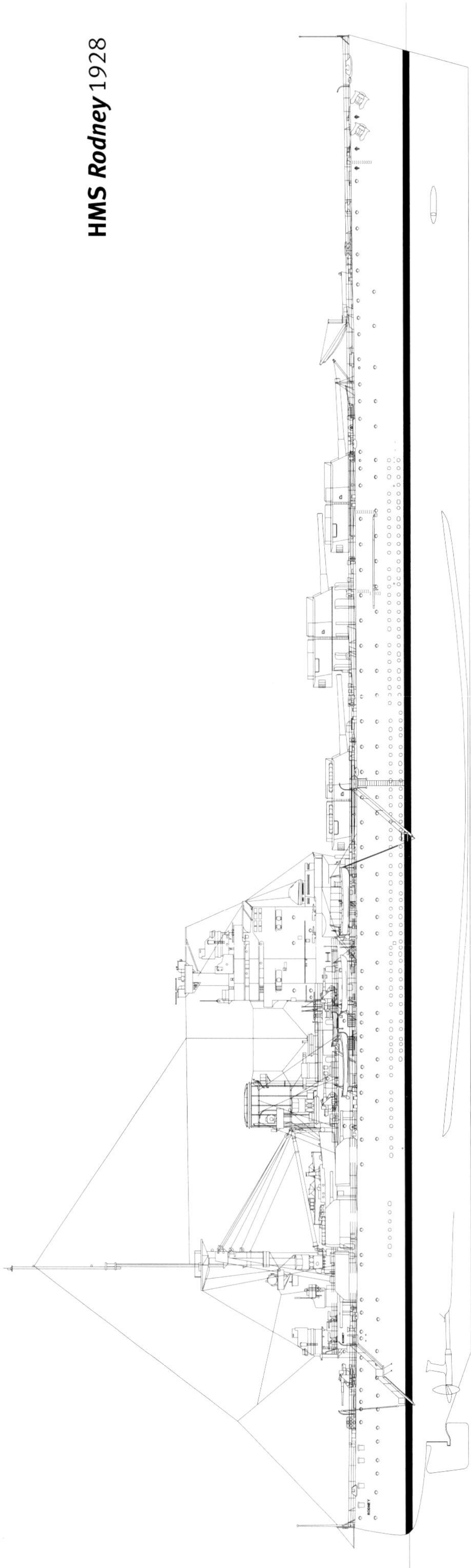

HMS *Rodney* 1928

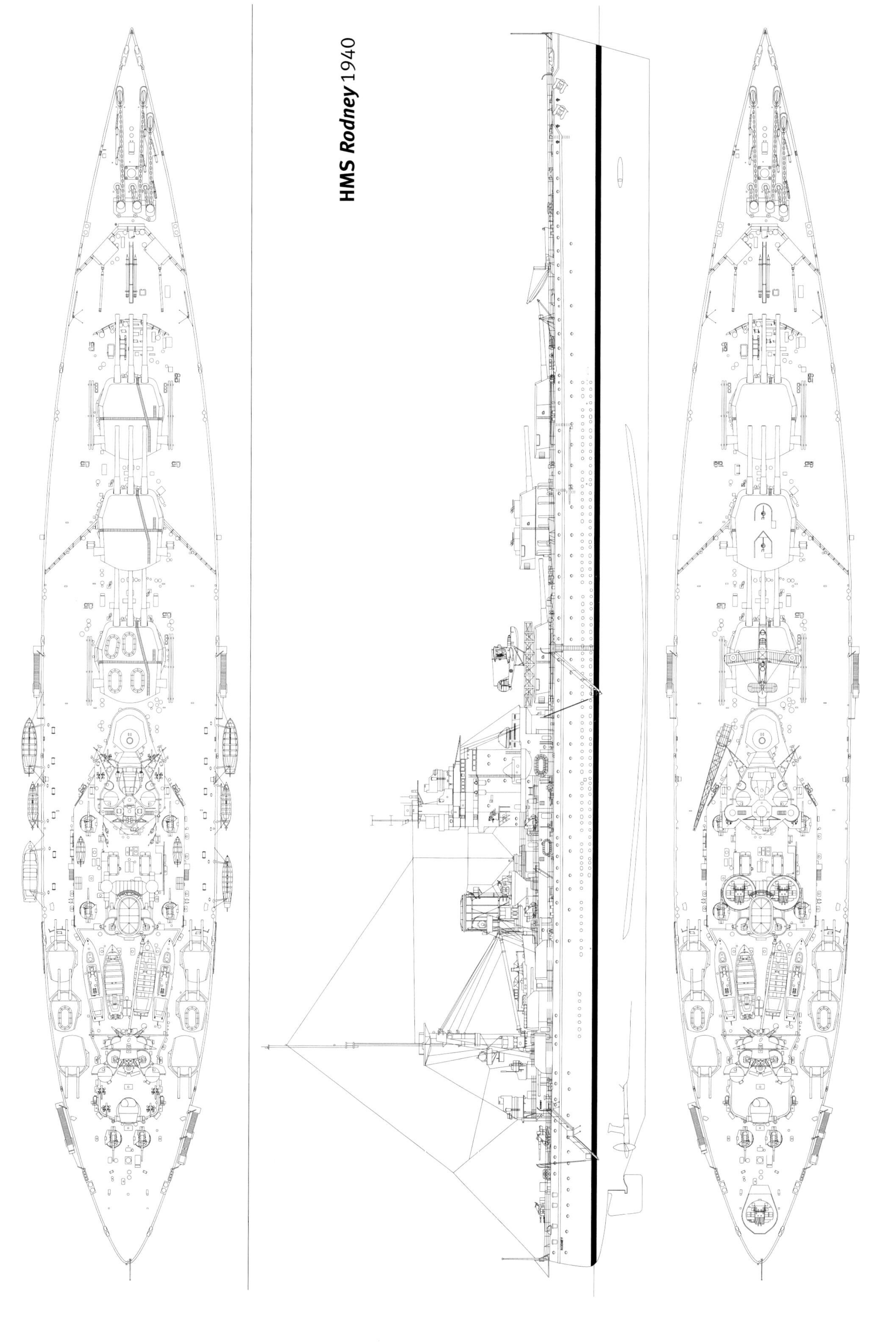

HMS *Rodney* 1940

HMS *Rodney* 1942

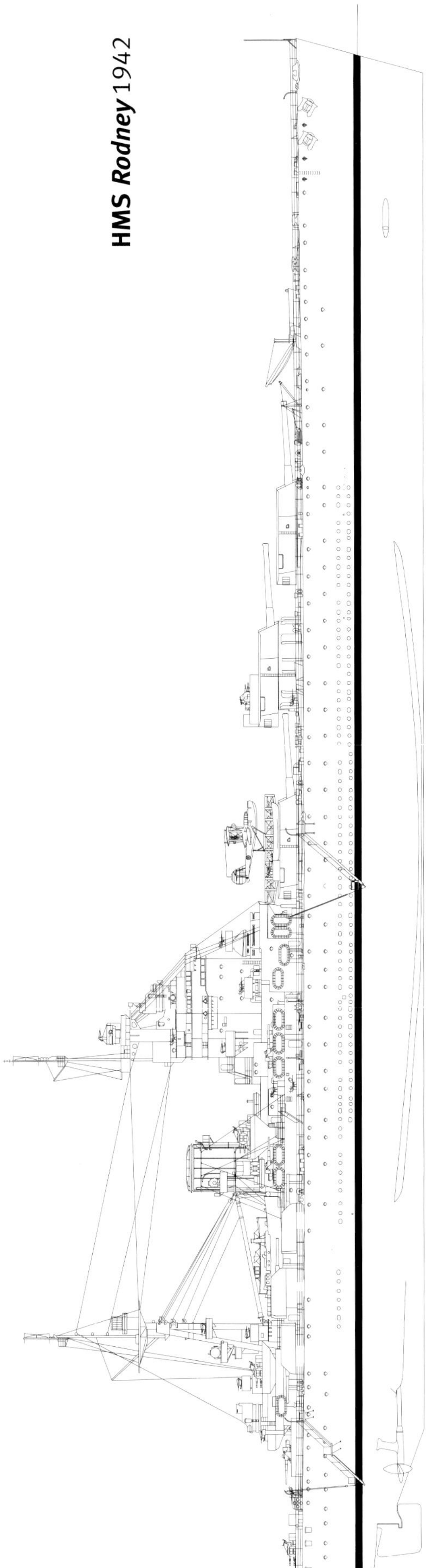

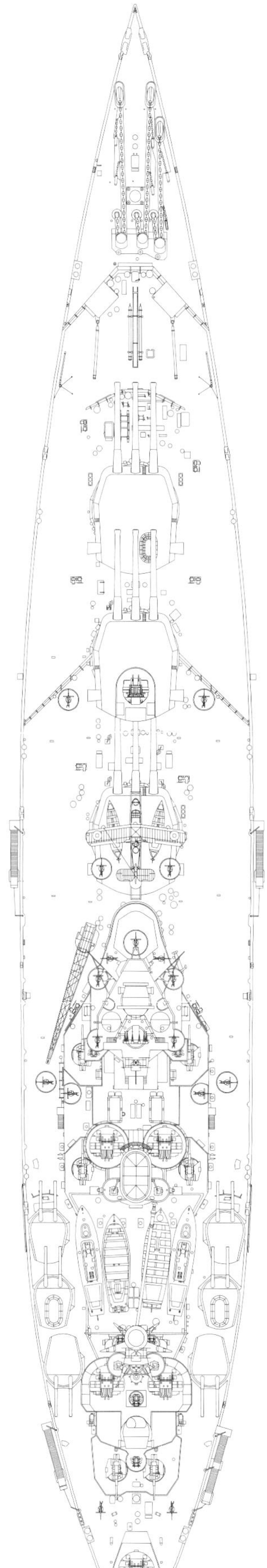

HMS *Rodney* 1944

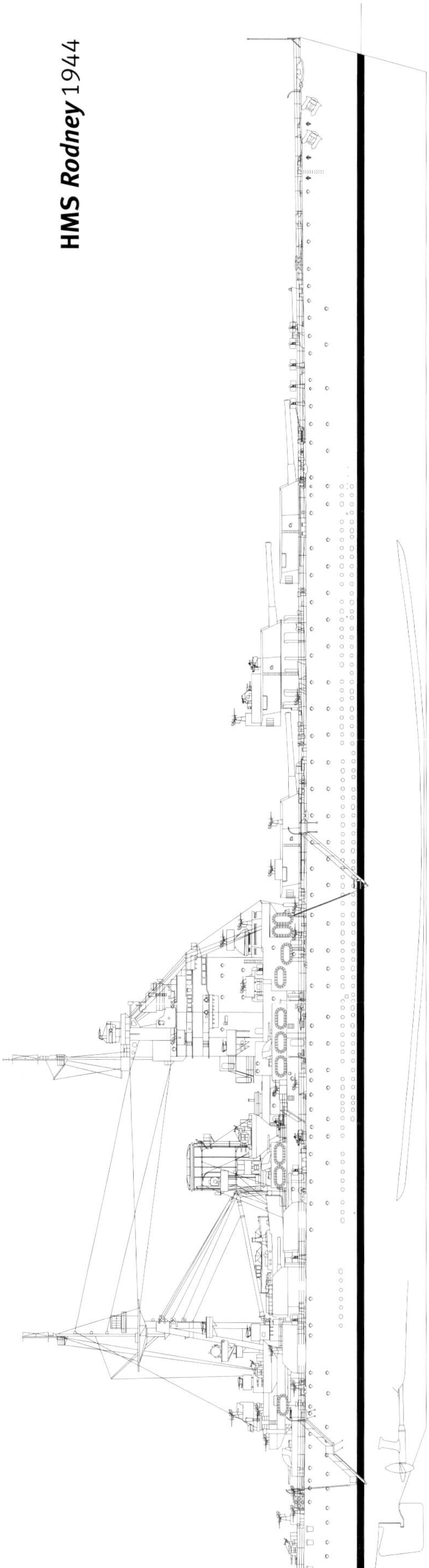

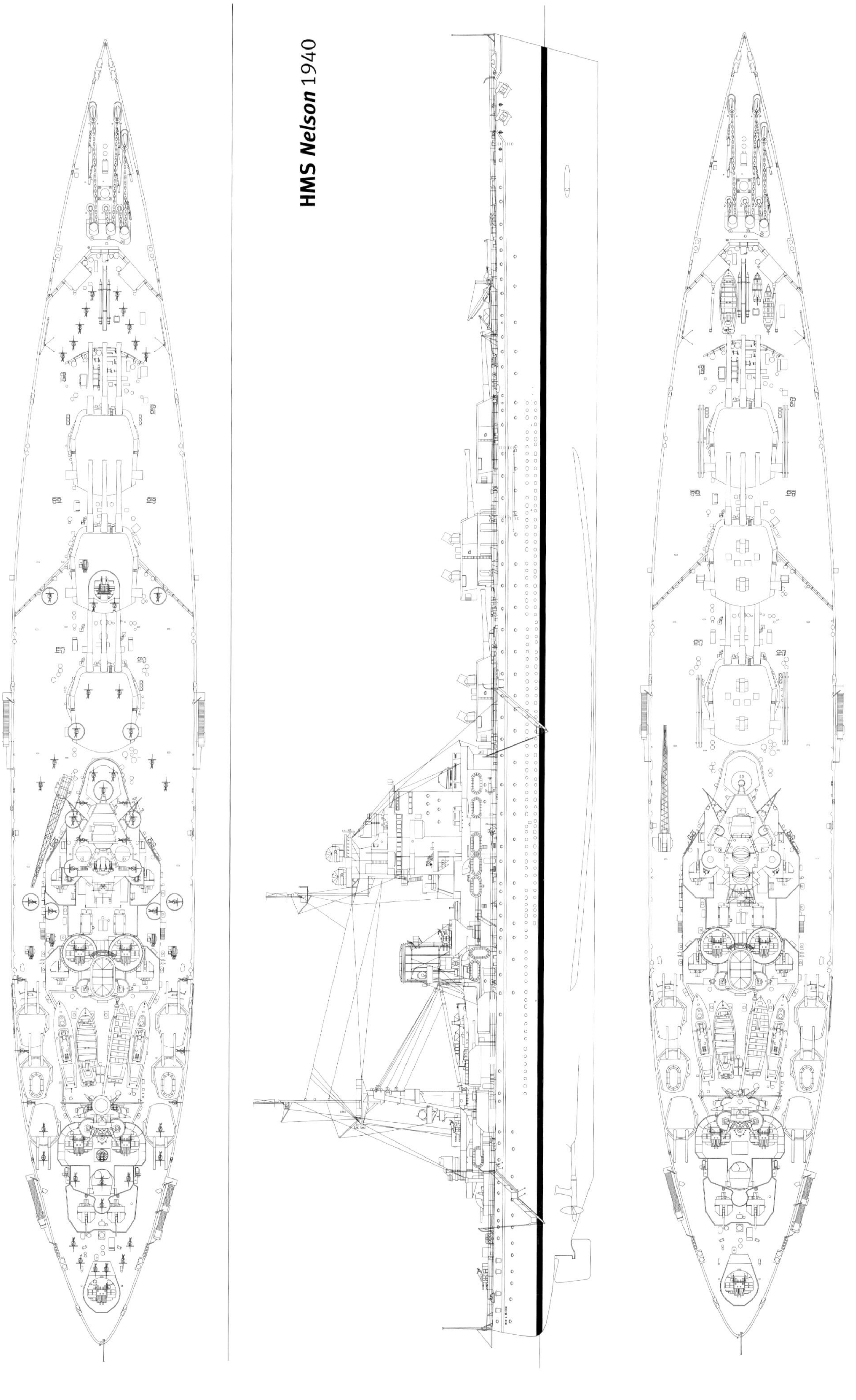

HMS *Nelson* 1940

HMS *Nelson* 1942

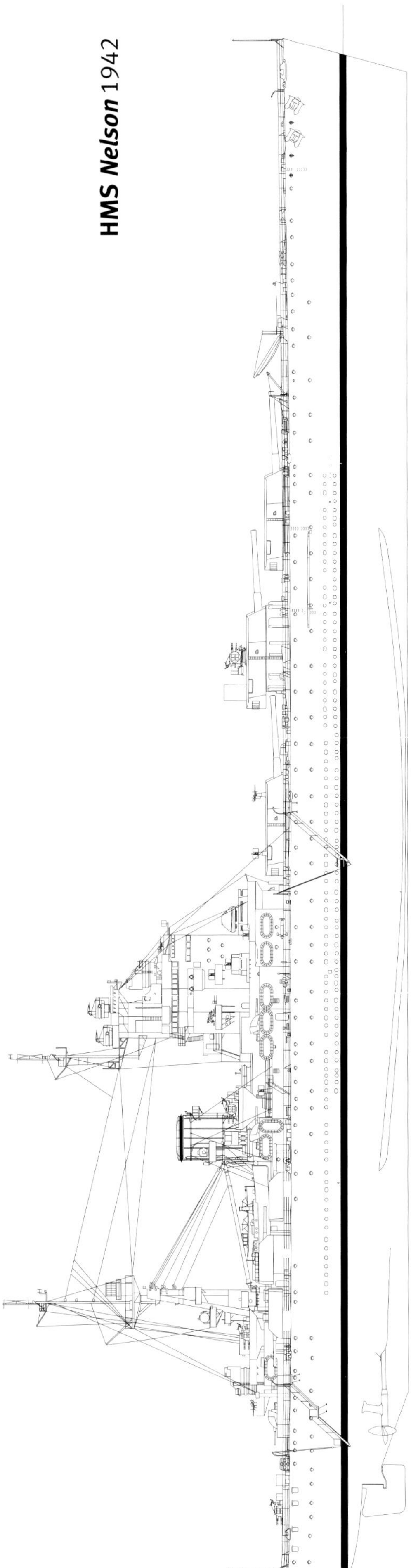

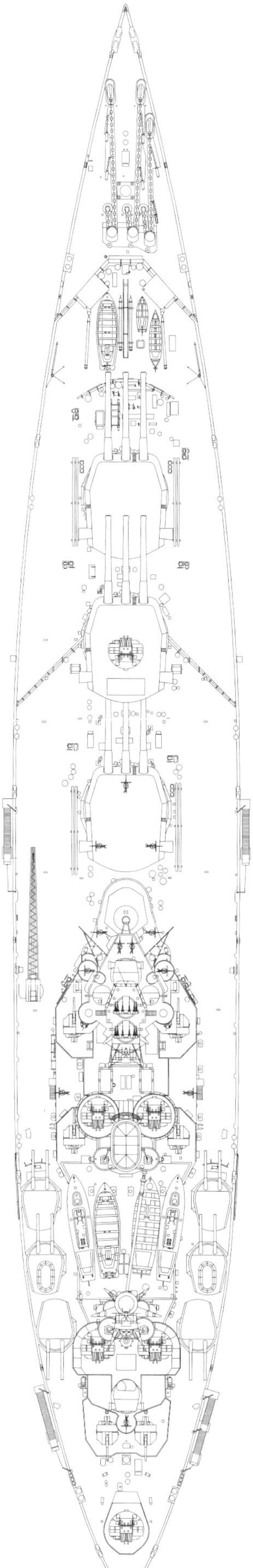

HMS *Nelson* 1943

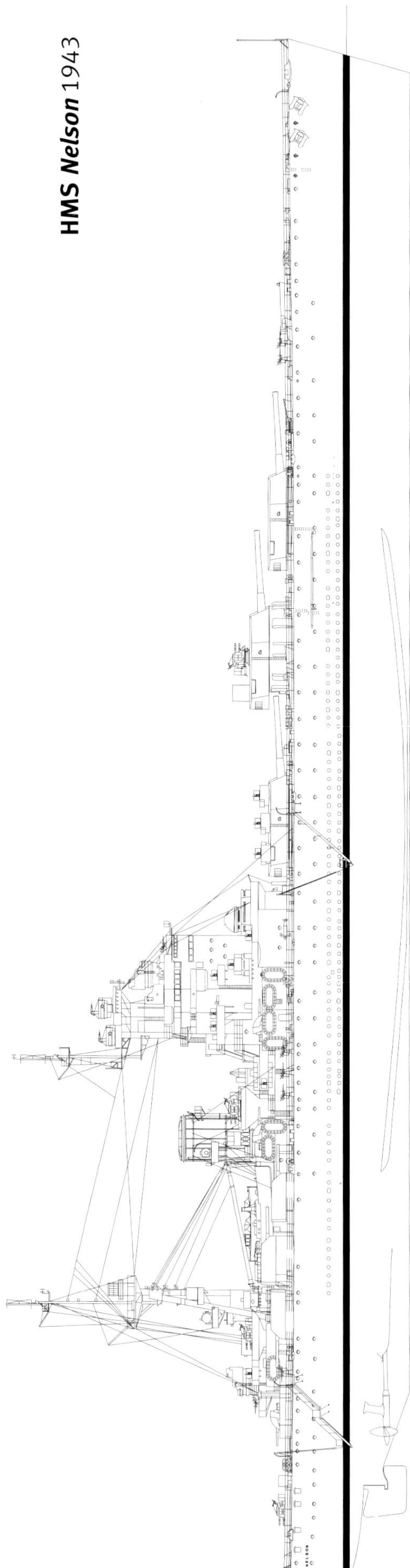

HMS *Nelson* 1945

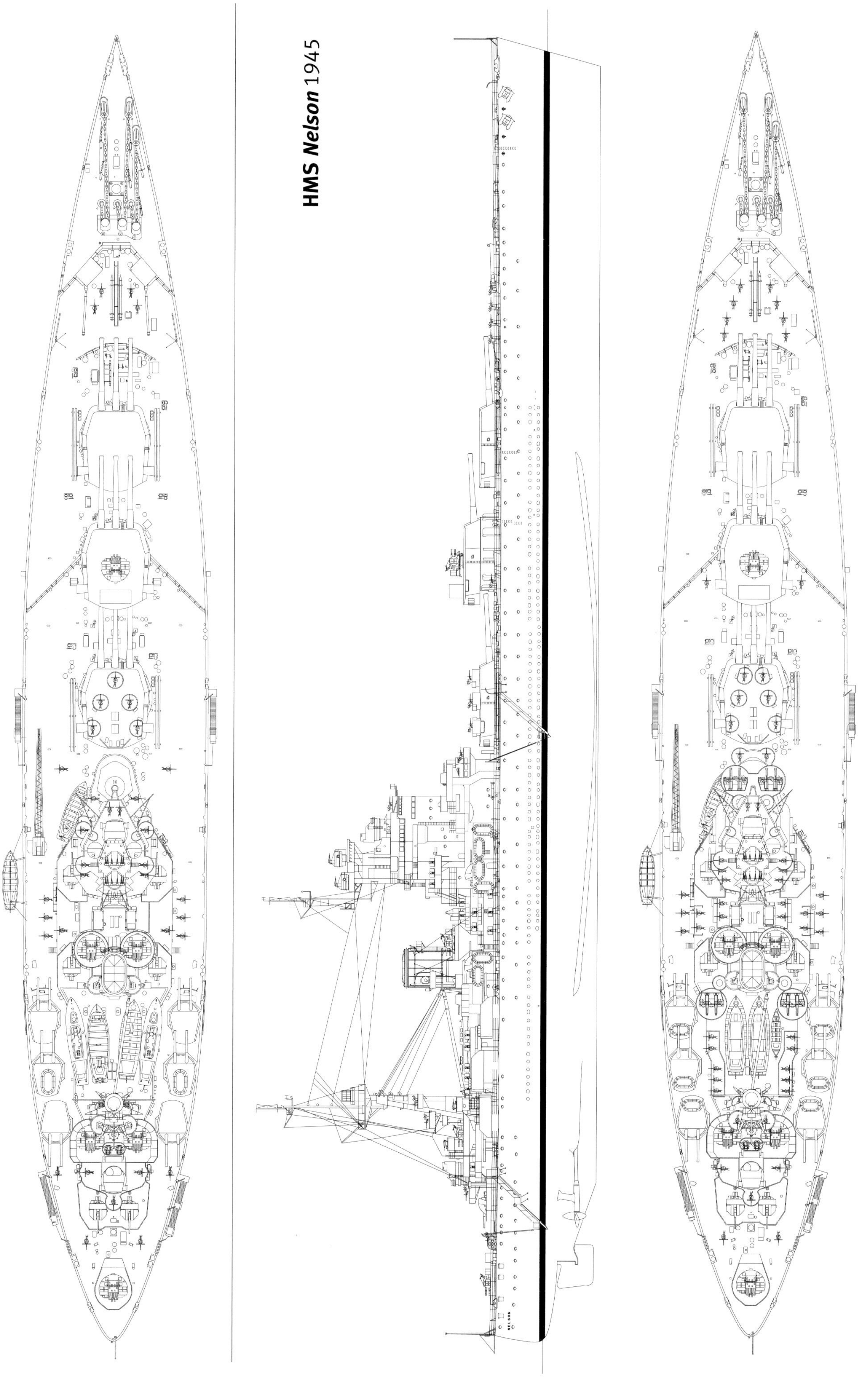

Selected References

REFERENCES

Brown, David K, *The Grand Fleet* (Chatham Publishing 1999). A look at the design of all Royal Navy warship types from 1905 to 1922. The design and construction of *Rodney* and *Nelson* are covered in detail.

Brown, David K, *Nelson to Vanguard* (Chatham Publishing 2000). A look at the design of all Royal Navy warship types from 1923 to 1945. Some good information about follow on battleship designs to *Rodney* and *Nelson*.

Brown, David K, 'Revolution Manqué', *Warship 1993* (Conway Maritime Press 1993). An account of the many innovative changes undertaken by the Royal Navy in the early 1920s.

Burt, R A, *British Battleships 1919-1945*, (Seaforth Publishing 2012). An excellent technical reference on all the Royal Navy's battleships and battlecruisers in service after the First World War. Contains a complete chapter on the design and construction of *Rodney* and *Nelson* with a very good analysis of the major damage suffered by *Nelson* during the Second World War. Very good reference drawings.

Campbell, N J M, 'Washington's Cherry Trees', *Warship Volume I* (Conway Maritime Press 1977). 4 part article on the evolution of the 'G3' and 'N3' designs.

Campbell, N J M, 'British Super-Heavy Guns Part 4', *Warship Volume III*, (Conway Maritime Press 1979). Many details on the construction of the 16in Mk I guns, the shells, and the gun linings.

Careless, Ronald, *Battleship Nelson* (Arms and Armour Press 1985). The wartime adventures of HMS *Nelson* from the viewpoint of the crew, with plenty of interesting anecdotes.

Cunningham, Andrew B Viscount Cunningham of Hyndhope, *A Sailor's Odyssey*, (Taylor Garnett Evans & Co 1951). The classic account of ABC's naval career from boy seaman to First Sea Lord, with a chapter of his experiences commanding *Rodney* in 1930.

Friedman, Norman, *US Battleships – An Illustrated Design History* (Naval Institute Press 1985). A detailed technical study of all US battleship designs, with some interesting observations about how US designers viewed the *Nelsons* as an 'impossible design'.

Hone, Trent, 'High-Speed Thoroughbreds: The US Navy's *Lexington* Class Battle Cruiser Designs', *Warship 2011* (Conway 2011). An analysis of the evolution of the design for the *Lexington* class battlecruisers, which were very much on the Admiralty's mind when the designs for the 'G3's were being developed.

Jordan, John, 'The Origins of *Dunkerque* and *Strasbourg*', *Warship 1999-2000* (Conway Maritime Press 1999). The design and construction of the French battlecruisers, which used many of the innovations pioneered in the *Nelsons*.

Raven, Alan, and Roberts, John, *Man o' War 3: Battleships Rodney and Nelson* (Arms and Armour Press 1979). The design and careers of *Rodney* and *Nelson*, with drawings, technical details, and many photos.

Raven, Alan, and Roberts, John, *British Battleships of World War Two* (Arms & Armour Press 1976). A very detailed technical reference to the Royal Navy's battleships and battlecruisers that saw service in the Second World War. There is a complete chapter devoted to the design and construction of *Rodney* and *Nelson*. Subsequent sections deal with modifications and war service. Still the definitive study.

Roberts, John, 'The Final Action – The Sinking of *Bismarck*, 27 May 1941', *Warship Volume VII* (Conway Maritime Press 1983). A very detailed account of the gunnery action between *King George V* and *Rodney* against *Bismarck* and an interesting comparison of the performance of the 16in and 14in guns.

INTERNET REFERENCES:

Nelson's Service History: http://www.naval-history.net/xGM-Chrono-01BB-HMS_Nelson.htm

Rodney's Service History:: http://www.naval-history.net/xGM-Chrono-01BB-HMS_Rodney.htm

MODEL MANUFACTURERS

ABER
ul. Jałowcowa 15, 40-750 Katowice, Poland
www.aber.net.pl

AIRFIX
Customer Care, Hornby Hobbies Ltd, Westwood, Margate, Kent CT9 4JX, United Kingdom. www.airfix.com

ALL WOOD SHIPS
www.allwoodships.com

ARTWOXMODEL
3F, No 877, Zhenhua Street, Fushan Area, Yantai City, Shandong Province, China. www.artwox.com

ATLAS EDITIONS
Route des Dragons 7, CH-1033 Cheseaux sur Lausanne, Switzerland. www.atlaseditions.co.uk

B&D BARRELS
Bruce Buchner, 6605 Winstead Manor Court,Lorton, VA 22079, USA bdbarrels.com

IRON SHIPWRIGHTS, INC
237 Gum Hollow Road, Oak Ridge, TN 37830, USA
www.ironshipwrights.com

MASTER PIOTR CZERKASOW
71-126 Szczecin, ul 26 Kwietnia 49/44, Poland
www.master-model.pl

MK1 DESIGN
KA-MODELS, B205 DaeRyung Post Tower 2nd, Guro3Dong, Guro-Gu, Seoul, Korea 152-790
www.ka-models.com

MOUNTFORD METAL MINIATURES
14 Cherry Tree Drive, Duckmanton, Chesterfield
S44 5JL, United Kingdom
www.mountfordmodels.com

NAVIS MODELLBAU
Dr I Kraus, Mozartweg 2, D-8538 Geretsried, Germany
www.navis-neptun.de

TAMIYA INCORPORATED
Shizuoka, Japan. www.tamiya.com

TOM'S MODELWORKS
8532 Lamar Drive, Huntington Beach, CA 92647, USA
www.tomsmodelworks.com

WHITE ENSIGN MODELS*
Unit 5, Cobnash Industrial Estate, Kingsland, Leominster HR6 9RW, United Kingdom. www.whiteensignmodels.com
*Tom's Modelworks was in the process of acquiring this business in early 2015.

WYDAWNICTWO JSC
Skrytka 20, 80-305 Gdańsk 5 Oliwa, Poland. www.jsc.pl

WYDAWNICTWO MODELIK
Janusz Oleś, 74-100 Gryfino, PO Box 145, Poland
www.modelik.pl